MIDDLE LEADERSHIP IN SCHOOLS

Middle Leadership in Schools: Ideas and Actions for Navigating the Muddy Waters of Middle Leading is a unique book in that it brings together practitioners, researchers, consultants, and administrators, to share their stories and ideas about middle leadership in schools. Thus, each chapter is both theoretically robust and pragmatically relevant. This is important because in each case the wisdom that is shared is reliable and relatable, and written in a style that is accessible to all. Middle leaders provide crucial leadership in schools – in and around classrooms where the purposes of education are enacted and fulfilled, so this is an important volume in that it provides needed professional learning for these key leaders. Furthermore, the chapters cover some of the fundamental practices of middle leadership, including the development and maintenance of trust, how to lead change and innovation through action research, and strategic thinking and planning. I commend the chapters in this book to school middle leaders, as important insights that can help you reflect upon, and develop, your own middle leading practices in your own educational site.

—*Peter Grootenboer*, Professor of Education,
Griffith University

Middle Leadership in Schools is a powerful guide that brilliantly illuminates the challenges and opportunities faced by middle leaders. With its diverse perspectives from across Australia, this book is an invaluable companion for anyone navigating the muddy waters of middle leading. I wish I had this treasure during my own middle leadership journey!

—*Lauren Sayer*, Director Curriculum Victorian
Curriculum Assessment Authority

This is a book for aspiring school middle leaders. It sets out the complexities of the role so that you will know what to expect.

It is valuable for current middle leaders. It illustrates the volatility of the job you're doing and help you understand why your job can be so tricky to carry out.

Senior leaders will benefit from reading it. It will assist you to unravel the challenges of getting the best from your organisation's middle layer.

The range of expertise on show makes this an easy to read yet thought-provoking book. It bridges the gap between the regularly criticised 'ivory tower' academic approach and purely anecdotal, bias laden non-generalisable accounts.

The structure is clear and ensures the reader thinks about the content. Guiding questions and reflective questions and tasks steer you though varying perspectives. Real-world experiences are supported and underpinned by academic citations. This is important when discussing crucial middle leader issues such as identity, trust and authenticity.

It is a book that has sought the opinion and critical appreciation of those doing this vital work in schools and robustly validated it. It works well.

It is an important addition to school middle leadership literature.

—*Bill Lowe*, Responsible for the design and delivery of Education Leadership in the Education MA at Newman University, Birmingham, UK. Author of *Middle Leadership for 21st Century Schools*. Crown House

Middle-level leadership is the engine room for positive change in a school. I have been privileged to work with Liz in the hard graft of positive school improvement from the middle and to learn from Barbara and Patrick's work over many years. I strongly recommend their thoughtful, expert and empathetic approach to bringing the best minds in middle leadership together in this essential book on building a thriving school and future for senior leadership.

—*Karen Money*, Regional Director Victorian Department of Education

MIDDLE LEADERSHIP IN SCHOOLS

Ideas and Strategies for Navigating the Muddy Waters of Leading from the Middle

EDITED BY

ELIZABETH BENSON
Pivotal Leadership, Australia

PATRICK DUIGNAN
Leading to Inspire, Australia

AND

BARBARA WATTERSTON
Australian Council for Educational Leaders, Australia

United Kingdom – North America – Japan
India – Malaysia – China

Emerald Publishing Limited
Emerald Publishing, Floor 5, Northspring, 21-23 Wellington Street,
Leeds LS1 4DL.

First edition 2024

British Library Cataloguing in Publication Data
A catalogue record for this book is available from the British Library

ISBN: 978-1-83753-085-4 (Print)
ISBN: 978-1-83753-082-3 (Online)
ISBN: 978-1-83753-084-7 (Epub)

CONTENTS

LIST OF FIGURES AND TABLES

Figures

Tables

ABOUT THE EDITORS

Elizabeth Benson firmly believes that 'every student deserves a great teacher, and every teacher deserves the opportunity to be great'. Throughout her career, she has been devoted to enhancing the capabilities of teachers and leaders in secondary schools. Her current focus lies in empowering middle leaders within schools, enabling them to thrive in their roles. To this end, she founded Pivotal Leadership, offering coaching and mentoring programs specifically tailored to middle leaders. In 2018, she established the Australian Council of Educational Leaders Queensland (ACELQ) Pivotal People Middle Leaders professional network, which serves as a valuable resource for educators in the middle leadership tier of educational institutions. She has amassed a wealth of experience in various roles, including Leadership Capability Development, Deputy Principal, and Pedagogy and Curriculum leader. She also wrote the Australian literature review for the AITSL Middle Leadership Environmental Scan. Currently pursuing a PhD at Griffith University, she is dedicated to investigating how middle leaders in secondary schools develop their leading practices. Her research aims to shed light on this crucial aspect of educational leadership.

Professor Emeritus Patrick Duignan has been involved in education for over 50 years as a Teacher, Deputy Principal, and Principal and in several positions from Lecturer to Professor and Dean in tertiary education institutions in several countries. He was Head of The Centre for Administrative Studies, University of New England; Professor Emeritus at Australian Catholic University, Australia; Past President of the Australian Council for Educational Leaders; Dean of the Faculty of Education, University Brunei Darussalam; and Director of Leading to Inspire. He received his initial university education at the National University of Ireland, Dublin (BA & Higher Diploma In Education) and then at the University of Alberta, Canada (BEd, MEd Admin and PhD).

Barbara Watterston has extensive experience in education and has held several executive leadership positions across Australia within the education and not-for-profit community sectors. She is currently the CEO of the Australian Council for Educational Leaders (ACEL). Her national and international research, consultancy, coaching, and speaking engagements centre on leadership development that emphasises the impact of high-quality leadership on providing the enabling conditions for all to thrive. Recognised for her contribution to educational leadership and professional learning, her national research report, *Insights: Environmental Scan Principal Preparation Programs* contributed to five major national recommendations for preparing future school leaders. Her doctoral thesis focused on gender, leadership, and learning, which informed her contribution as Co-editor of the book *Women in School Leadership: Journeys to Success*, and, more recently, *Step In, Step Up: Empowering Women for the School Leadership Journey* with co-author Jane Kise, which received a Silver Medal in the 2020 IBPA Benjamin Franklin Awards. Recognised for her contributions to leadership and professional learning, she was the Inaugural Recipient of the Women of Achievement Award (WA DoE), a National Fellow of ACEL, and an Honorary Fellow of the Melbourne Graduate School of Education.

ABOUT THE CONTRIBUTORS

Samuel Alexeeff has worked in education full-time since 2014. During his teaching career, he has taught across primary schools, remote community schools, and senior high schools in Western Australia. He has held various middle leadership positions including Curriculum Leader, Year Leader, and Program Coordinator in Behaviour Management. He has also recently held acting Principal positions in two remote community schools.

Danielle Cioffi has been a High School teacher in South Australia for the past 12 years. She has taught English, Humanities, and Legal Studies from 7 to 12 and has recently been appointed to a Director of High School Curriculum position. She received her Bachelor of Arts and Secondary Education from Tabor Adelaide and her Master of Education, with a Gifted Education specialisation, from Flinders University. She is a SACE Legal Studies subject expert, and in 2021, co-authored a Year 12 textbook titled, *SACE 2 – Legal Studies*, on the subject, available through Essentials Education.

Emma Dearing is a Curriculum Leader (Literacy and Mathematics) in a remote country primary school. Her other middle leadership roles have included Acting Deputy Principal and Curriculum Leader in Mathematics. Developing whole school plans, liaising with school administration, instructional coaching, and fortnightly curriculum meetings with year-level team to analyse student data form a large part of her current role.

Christine Edwards-Groves is Professor and Research Fellow at Griffith University, Australia. Formerly, she was an Experienced Teacher and Middle Leader, and now a Teacher Educator and Researcher. She has almost four decades of experience researching and working in national and international contexts. She researches literacy practices, dialogic pedagogies, and middle leadership, and has expertise in practice theory (specifically, the theory of practice architectures) and action research. Currently, she is a Chief Investigator in a study examining the impact of middle leadership on student learning. She is widely published in the field of middle leadership, and has three co-authored books on middle leadership including *Middle Leadership in Schools: A Practical Guide for Leading Learning* (Grootenboer, Edwards-Groves, and Rönnerman, 2020), *Generative Leadership: Rescripting the Promise of Action Research* (Edwards-Groves and Rönnerman, 2021), and *Leading From the Middle – Teachers Driving Professional Development* (in Swedish, Rönnerman, Edwards-Groves, and Grootenboer, 2018).

Sarah Gunn currently holds the position of Director of Studies and Pedagogy at St Peters Lutheran College Springfield, a co-educational, Lutheran P-12 school in Queensland, Australia. She recently completed her Master of Educational Leadership, focusing her literature review on the practices of highly effective professional learning communities (PLCs). She is passionate about leveraging contemporary educational research to lead practical, impactful, and context-specific school improvement initiatives. She is particularly interested in cultures of thinking, learner agency, and inquiry-based professional collaboration. She is also passionate about contributing to the profession across educational sectors through her work with Pivotal People, a professional learning network run by middle leaders, for middle leaders.

Michael Harrison is a Senior Learning Lead, Leadership Development, Melbourne Archdiocese Catholic Schools (MACS). He has extensive experience of teaching and leading in three Catholic secondary schools in the Archdiocese of Melbourne and has degrees in Arts, Theology, and Religious Education. His current interest is the exploration of how the leadership of Catholic schools can respond positively to the many challenges facing Catholic schools today.

Steven Kolber works within the Faculty of Education at the University of Melbourne. Previously, he was an English Language teacher within a government school for the past 12 years. In 2021, he was named a top 50 finalist in the Varkey Foundation's Global Teacher Prize. He has represented teachers globally for Education International, at the International Labour Organisation (ILO), the OECDs Global Teaching Insights, and UNESCOs Teacher Task Force 2030. His research explores teacher empowerment, professional learning, pedagogy, andragogy, teacher research engagement, activism, and social media. His recent book with Dr Keith Heggart, *Empowering Teachers and Democratising Schooling: Perspectives From Australia,* considers many possibilities for ways to develop and improve teacher status.

Jenny Lewis is an experienced National and International Education Advisor and provides leadership coaching and facilitation roles for international, national, and state education systems to develop innovative, performance-focused sustainable practices. Recognised for her expertise in leadership capability development, she has co-designed school and system leadership development continuums, frameworks, and learning maps for the Australian Council for Educational Leaders, the Commonwealth of Nations, and most recently the Worldwide Innovation Summit for Education. She is an Education Advisor to the Indonesia Ministry of Education, Culture, Research and Technology Director-Generals Schools and Teacher Quality. She was the Lead Author along with Liz in completing the AITSL Middle Leadership Environmental Scan that detailed evidence regarding middle leader impact in Australian schools, international application of middle leadership standards, and recommendations regarding future work to support middle leadership development. She is currently completing her PhD and is analysing international principal preparation certification and registration programs with an aim to building an evidence-led program for Australian aspirant principals.

Kylie Lipscombe is an Associate Professor at the University of Wollongong. She is an Australian researcher, educator, and presenter with nearly 25 years' experience in schools, school systems and universities. Kylie has contributed to international, national, and state educational initiatives and policy in middle leadership, leadership development, and teacher collaboration. She has authored numerous books, book chapters, journal articles and government reports. She is the academic leader for the NSW Department of Education (NSW DoE) Senior Leader- Aspiring Principals Program, and NSW DoE Middle Leadership Development Program. Currently she is on the advisory board to the Australian Institute for Teaching & School Leadership (AITSL) development of The Professional Standards for Middle Leaders and serves as the President of ACEL NSW and Deputy President of ACEL nationally.

Pamela Macklin has held several senior positions in Australian education. She is an experienced Senior Executive, Coach, Teacher, Education Consultant, and Writer. Most recently, she co-authored the highly successful *Driving School Improvement: Practical Strategies and Tools* (2nd ed.) with Vic Zbar. She has significant experience in the development and management of major community and education projects. Her interests lie in leadership coaching, the management of organisational change and improvement, educational policy, curriculum, assessment, and school improvement. Her national and international work has focused on education reform and has included the development of policy and implementation strategies in areas such as ICT in education, literacy, numeracy, studies of Asia, and gender equity. She is also an experienced Company Director and has held several positions on not-for-profit boards.

Wendy McKay is a Head of Department for Queensland Hospital Education Programs. She leads curriculum improvement with several teaching teams in mental health programs across the Southeast Region. She started her school career as a Primary School Teacher, quickly moving into middle leadership roles at the local level before accepting Senior Educational Officer roles at the regional level, working with over 100 state schools on curriculum improvement. She has her Masters in Educational Leadership and Management, and has continued to leverage this qualification over the years to develop models and processes for curriculum innovation and improvement specific to school systems, group of and individual schools, middle leadership teams, and teacher practitioner needs.

Professor Donna Pendergast is the Director of Engagement in the Arts, Education and Law Group and Former Dean and Head of the School of Education and Professional Studies at Griffith University. Her research expertise is education transformation and efficacy, with a focus on middle year's education and student engagement, early years, initial and professional teacher education, and school reform. She commenced her career as a schoolteacher working in secondary, P-10 and senior college settings before shifting to the role of academic at Queensland University of Technology, The University of Queensland, and since 2009, at Griffith University. She has served in roles associated with the profession at state and federal government levels. She has more than 170 refereed publications along with 23 books including the highly regarded *Teaching Middle Years: Rethinking Curriculum, Pedagogy, and Assessment*, now in its fourth edition.

Danny Pinchas has more than 15 years' experience as a Leader across the education sector and joined AITSL in 2013. As General Manager, Teaching and School Leadership, he leads AITSL's work across initial teacher education reform, quality teaching support, and school leadership development. His responsibilities involve driving and supporting the development and implementation of a range of policy initiatives and resources to empower teachers and school leaders. Prior to joining AITSL, he held positions at the Victorian Department of Education and before that spent several years in the Kimberley region of Western Australia, working in remote communities as a principal, teacher, and numeracy coach.

Jessica Pound is an experienced teacher specialising in Physical Education, Health, Dance, and Literacy in both primary and secondary settings. She is particularly interested in improving the education outcomes for students in regional areas, including in geographically remote First Nations Aboriginal communities in the Northern Territory, where she worked on curriculum development for a brief period. She is currently a Specialist Literacy Teacher and School-based Middle Leader facilitating school development in literacy education.

Louisa Rennie is General Manager of Leadership Development at Melbourne Archdiocese Catholic Schools (MACS). She is invested in the design, implementation, and evaluation of leadership pathways within a broader pipeline of organisational development that cater to and inspire leaders to flourish. She has a Master in Instructional Leadership and has worked across Catholic, independent, and government systems in Australia and internationally. She is Co-author of the book *I'm the Principal; Principal Learning, Action, Influence and Identity*, published through ACER Press. She is passionate about leadership learning for continuous improvement, leadership performance standards, and leading change.

Stephanie Salazar is a Teacher, Assistant Principal, and Instructional Coach at John Purchase Public School. She is the Founder of the New Teacher Tribe initiative and #PSTchat, a Twitter chat dedicated to supporting pre-service teachers around the world. Her passion is inspiring educators to see more in themselves and their students. In 2022, she was a Commonwealth Bank Teaching Award fellow. She was awarded the Young Professional Award 2018 by the Australian College of Educators. In 2017, she also won the Executive Director's Recognition Award for Innovation and Creativity in Leading Learning Towards Improved Student Outcomes. She is passionate about building up new teachers, through middle leaders, so that we can all focus on doing spectacular work for our students.

Jodie Schafer has been teaching secondary students in Queensland for 30 years and has also taught in British Colombia Canada. She is currently Head of Humanities Faculty at Wavell. She has also worked in various curriculum roles with Queensland Curriculum and Assessment Authority. She studied her Bachelor of Arts and Graduate Diploma of Education at Griffith University, Queensland, Australia.

Nichole Tiller has been a Secondary Teacher, in South Australia for 14 years, and prior to that, she taught certificate courses in Vocational Education and Training to Year 11 and 12 students. She is currently the Director of Senior School Student Development at Cedar College. She oversees student leadership and a staff well-being initiative at her school and is passionate about supporting women in leadership within Christian Education. She has a Bachelor of Science, Bachelor of Education (middle/secondary), and a Master of Education.

Sharon Tindall-Ford is an Associate Professor of Educational Leadership in the School of Education at the University of Wollongong. She has worked as a Secondary Teacher and taught and researched in Educational Psychology for over 20 years. Her recent work focuses on school middle leadership and professional learning for school leaders in social emotional educational leadership.

Lucy Warnock is the Dedicated Well-being Coordinator at Immanuel College, in Adelaide, South Australia. As an Educator who has held multiple middle leadership positions since early in her career, her experience in both government and independent schools is extensive. Prior to her well-being role at Immanuel, she was Y8 Year-Level Coordinator for 12 years and has also been Acting Head of Middle School, numerous times since 2012. With a passion for helping students navigate the complexities of adolescence, she has been the leader in transforming the well-being curriculum. She has developed a bespoke framework and curriculum that includes a range of innovative programs that focus on respectful relationships, consent, and building resilience. Her warm and empathic approach has earned her the respect and credibility of students, colleagues, and the wider college community. She studied her Bachelor of Education (upper primary/lower secondary) at Flinders University.

FOREWORD
Dr Lyn Sharratt

This book, *Middle Leadership in Schools*, is a gift. The authors have brought together voices from all sectors in education contributing to the book's practicality and authenticity.

If leadership is defined in the Educational Administration literature as 'influence and impact', then middle leaders are in a strong position to influence and guide their colleagues in the never-ending pursuit of excellence and equity. The former being the growth and achievement of every learner and the latter meaning the inclusivity of ALL learners achieving success – and I really do mean ***all***. Middle leaders are educators intricately enmeshed in the leading of professional learning (PL) and teaching practices in their schools – downward, outward, and upward. They are the essential glue, the critical link.

My research reveals that leaders establish the conditions for success in systems and schools – and that first condition in enabling and establishing the necessary linkages embraces 'relational trust', as multiple authors in this text so aptly point out. I concur that the ideal middle leader's identity includes the ability to reach staff members' consensus on a shared vision, on motivating and mobilising teachers to own that vision and on garnering a commitment to the vision. This facet of middle leader identity contributes to their power to make a difference.

This book is a must-read for all teachers and leaders – as everyone is a middle leader – 'leading from the middle' somewhere in their systems. Being very practical, it does not shy away from the challenges but offers heaps of practical guidance for aspiring middle leaders on approaching and overcoming the challenges.

I judge a book by what I have learned that can be implemented tomorrow – and this book hits that mark! It offers so many practical self-help suggestions. For example, 'soft tactics' to build trust – an imperative for middle leaders – are explained in detail, for instance: one-to-one conferencing with new staff members; buddying-up staff to work in pairs on staff members' 'next best learning moves'; co-constructing operating norms to cement respectful treatment of each other during every meeting; giving time to teachers to share their 'practices that work'; honouring work-life balance with no emails on weekends, holidays, and after 6 p.m. (and before 8 a.m.!). Authentic middle leaders work 'alongside' and learn the work while doing the work with their peers. Again, they are the glue.

Reflective questions sprinkled thoughtfully throughout this book help readers self-assess their next steps in developing and embracing their leadership identity. I am delighted with the focus on PL programs for middle leaders. Too often, the middle leader sector is not a valued focus for PL – in my opinion a grave omission.

I appreciate the authenticity of the narratives captured from middle leaders doing this leadership work. Middle leaders write that they are visible in classrooms, they work alongside teachers and students, they are expert teachers, and they are the conduit between the system vision and the schools moving forward to capture that vision. These middle leaders describe the opportunities they have had to not only engage with their teaching force but also to empower them to ensure that every learner is growing and achieving – beyond what their teachers and schools might ever have thought was possible. That, for me, is the essence and beauty of this must-read!

Commitment, communication, co-construction of meaning, clarity, and collaboration – the skills that middle leaders develop over time – are highlighted from each author's unique perspective in this book – how refreshing! 'Establishing Trust' is the middle leaders' foundation that underpins the work of system and school improvement. Thought-provoking and challenging as it is to build trust, middle leaders know that trust is built differently in differing contexts. Building trust is the first step in the puzzle to be solved by middle leaders, and fortunately for readers, this process is unpacked in this book.

Throughout this gem, we are constantly reminded that we must focus on the 'how' of purposeful collaboration and on the processes, structures, protocols, and tools that middle leaders use to:

✓ co-construct and test solutions;
✓ facilitate quality conversations;
✓ promote clarity;
✓ deepen connections; and
✓ celebrate all large and small wins.

Together, these approaches as implemented by middle leaders and teams, in authentic ways, sustain and accelerate the speed of change and progress for all students' growth and achievement (Clarke & Sharratt, 2023).

In conclusion, this book effectively researches and emphasizes the necessity for ***all*** leaders to support middle leaders actively, strategically, and intentionally, and give them the time, guidance, and PL they need to navigate the complex educational landscape that they find themselves in. It is worth the investment in building the capacity of middle leaders as they are the glue, we need to improve our systems and schools.

Brief Bio for Lyn
Dr Lyn Sharratt is a highly sought-after expert in the field of education. As a distinguished practitioner, researcher, author, and presenter, she has dedicated her career to turning cutting-edge research into practical guidance for school leaders and teachers. Based on her extensive experience and expertise, she has developed the CLARITY Learning Suite (CLS), a unique online roadmap for educational leaders and teachers. Through CLS, members learn to utilise ongoing assessment to inform instruction to 'Put FACES on the Data' and drive Equity and Excellence at all levels of the education system.

INTRODUCTION

Elizabeth Benson[a], Patrick Duignan[b] and Barbara Watterston[c]

[a]*Pivotal Leadership, Gold Coast, Queensland, Australia*
[b]*Leading to Inspire, Gold Coast, Queensland, Australia*
[c]*Australian Council for Educational Leaders, Sydney, NSW, Australia*

THE SCHOOL MIDDLE LEADERSHIP CONTEXT

Schools, education systems, and academics are currently investigating who are middle leaders, what do they do, how to best develop middle leader capability, and what is the impact of middle leadership on student learning. However, very little middle leader voice can be found in any of these conversations. This edited book aims to fill that gap and amplify the voice of middle leaders by sharing their leading practice.

Research into what middle leaders do is starting to highlight the complex nature of leading from the middle. Leadership research in schools has tended to focus primarily on principals and the principalship, and the attention given to middle leadership by researchers and education systems has, for the most part, been on strengthening the pool of potential principals and therefore the succession of middle leaders to the principalship. This book gives primary attention to the leadership of middle leaders by including them as authors or co-authors of various chapters. In doing so, this book positions middle leadership as a worthy leadership career in its self and amplifies the voice of middle leaders in deepening our collective understanding of educational leadership.

There is no clear definition of a middle leader in literature, research, or policy. Middle leaders can be described by:

- positionality;
- formality of role; and/or
- tasks and accountabilities.

It would be pertinent of a middle leader or principal to reflect on these three features of middle leadership in their school context as middle leaders are different from teacher leaders and principals (Grootenboer et al., 2020; Lipscombe et al., 2021). Middle leaders have been defined as 'those who assume formal responsibilities and duties of leadership and management at a level situated between principal and teachers' (Li et al., 2021, p. 2). This definition creates a picture of the position a middle leader holds in an organisational hierarchy. Middle leaders who authored chapters in this book might find Grootenboer et al.'s (2020) definition of middle leadership closer to their reality: middle leaders hold formal leadership responsibilities and significant teaching responsibilities. 'It is middle leaders who have some positional responsibility to bring about change in their schools, yet maintain close connections to the classroom as sites where student learning occurs' (Grootenboer et al., 2020, p. 2). There are also middle leaders whose context is formal but not situated in a school. These middle leaders often work with other school leaders to support the development of education policy and practice within a system. The variety of middle leading positions, roles, and accountabilities adds to the complex nature of middle leadership.

From the relevant literature and the experience of the contributors to this book, it would appear that responsibility for leading school improvement is being distributed (or delegated) down the school hierarchy. However, we know very little about the impact of middle leadership on student learning, and it is also challenging to accurately capture the impact of middle leader practice (Lipscombe et al., 2021).

Many of the middle leaders who have contributed to this book are or have been responsible for driving school improvement in various roles, especially in a curriculum role, as a leader of pastoral care, leading whole-school improvement, or developing policy for a system. They provide insights into how they have led school improvement by connecting their practice to research. And while this book does not attempt to directly explore the impact of middle leadership on student learning, it does provide guidance and examples of how middle leaders can tackle some of the challenges of leading improvement in school.

Most middle leaders are, however, *leaders AND teachers*, and the themes in this book recognise the dualities that *exist* in school middle leadership. The chapters are organised around three themes:

- leading others AND empowering yourself;
- collaborating AND communicating; and
- leading learning AND leading change for improvement.

The inclusion of AND in each theme positions the middle leader as one who juggles the multiple responsibilities and roles of leading from the middle. When writing or contributing to a chapter in this book, middle leaders were requested to impart their wisdom about:

- their experiences as a middle leader;
- ideas and strategies for leading from the middle; and
- what changes are necessary to enable them to empower themselves, grow, and bloom as leaders.

When reflecting on their development needs within the chapters of this book, middle leaders suggest that the following are significant challenges for them:

- having difficult conversations, including navigating accountability and developing trusting relationships;
- leading strategically in a demanding environment, including leading school improvement, implementing a raft of school and

policy changes, and influencing others while responding to the daily challenges of school life; and

- developing the capability of teachers while finding opportunities to develop their own teaching practice and discovering their authentic leadership self.

As editors, we are encouraging middle leaders to use their professional artistry when dealing with challenging and messy situations. They need to be creative and resourceful when responding to new and unique problems that they haven't faced before, and they should be encouraged to 'invent' new ways of thinking and doing in responding to complex challenges. Successful middle leaders learn and grow each day, and they encourage others to do the same, that is, they empower others to become better leaders. By engaging with the stories of practice within this book, middle leaders can gain ideas on how they could craft unique responses to their unique challenges.

WHY A BOOK WRITTEN FOR AND BY MIDDLE LEADERS?

As editors, we had three goals for this book:

1. provide an opportunity for middle leaders to tell their story of 'middle leading' and add their voice to the existing literature about leading from the middle in schools – something that is currently weak or absent;
2. empower middle leaders to confidently tackle the challenges of middle leading informed by and through stories of other middle leaders; and
3. provide mentoring opportunities for middle leaders to develop their writing skills and confidence, hopefully empowering them to own their leadership voice.

The middle leaders who have contributed to this book have been chosen carefully to ensure thoughtful representation of the depth and breadth of middle leadership in schools. You will notice chapter authors from government, Catholic, and independent education sectors and from across Australia. Many of the middle leaders in schools are also classroom teachers. There are middle leaders included from primary and secondary schools; leaders who have significant years of leadership experience and others are earlier in their leadership career. We thank them for taking up this challenge, juggling their leading, teaching and writing, and sharing their leadership story with others.

Many of the middle leaders had never written for publication before, so we paired them with an experienced author or academic (or both). The role of the mentor was to guide the middle leader through the writing process. How that appeared in practice was different for each writing partnership, but our hope is that both the mentor and the middle leader have benefitted from this process. We thank Kylie Lipscombe, Sharon Tindall-Ford, Louisa Rennie, Pamela Macklin, and Donna Pendergast for their mentoring roles.

Each of the middle leaders who contributed to this edited collection took on the challenge of writing about aspects of their leadership. As a collection, their writings provide an overview of the sophisticated nature of middle leadership. The overview clearly indicates that middle leaders are:

- thinking and planning strategically;
- interpreting sophisticated curriculum and making decisions with their teams about what is best for the students in their context;
- cultivating safe cultures for teachers to talk about their practice and develop themselves as educators;
- researching teaching and learning using high-level action research skills;
- using data and evidence to diagnose problems of practice and collaborating with others to find solutions;
- shaping a clear sense of their leadership identity, being strategic and intentional about their own leadership development, and leveraging their strengths to create trusting learning environments;

- developing networks with educators outside their school to deepen knowledge of their craft;
- balancing the demands of senior leaders and teachers;
- influencing up, down, and across the school and system hierarchy;
- gathering the resources so that teachers can provide learning experiences that engage students;
- using their organisation and management skills to manage their workload and the workload of their team; and
- understanding and recognising their impact and ensuring they are leading with integrity and authenticity.

THE STRUCTURE OF THIS BOOK

The topics represented in this book have been chosen based on the research into what middle leaders do, the challenges they face, and the passions that inspire them to lead. Each chapter explores an aspect of three dualities of middle leadership:

- leading others AND empowering self;
- collaborating AND communicating; and
- leading learning AND leading change for improvement.

Each chapter starts with guiding questions to stimulate reflection on the reader's own leading practices. Within each chapter, the authors provide reflection questions or tasks, practical examples, or vignettes of practice to further enhance the reader's learning experience. The editors are confident that middle leaders will find the wisdom and advice given on leadership by the authors valuable for improving their leadership practices within their spheres of influence. We hope you enjoy reading this book and find its content practical, informative, and inspiring.

REFERENCES

Grootenboer, P., Edwards-Groves, C., & Rönnerman, K. (2020). *Middle leadership in schools: A practical guide for leading learning*. Routledge.

Li, S. C., Poon, A. Y. K., Lai, T. K. H., & Tam, S. T. C. (2021). Does middle leadership matter? Evidence from a study of system-wide reform on English language curriculum. *International Journal of Leadership in Education*, *24*(2), 226–243.

Lipscombe, K., Tindall-Ford, S., & Lamanna, J. (2021). School middle leadership: A systematic review. *Educational Management Administration and Leadership*, *19*(1), 1–19.

LEADING OTHER AND EMPOWERING YOURSELF

1

MIDDLE LEADER IDENTITY

Samuel Alexeeff[a], Emma Dearing[a], Kylie Lipscombe[b] and Sharon Tindall-Ford[b]

[a]*Department of Education, Perth, WA, Australia*
[b]*University of Wollongong, Wollongong, NSW, Australia*

ABSTRACT

This chapter explores middle leadership identity through the real-world accounts of how two middle leaders construct and develop their leadership identity and how this impacts the way their middle leadership is practiced. Leadership identity, an internal narrative of oneself as a leader which is practised professionally in context, represents a concept that is best understood as being unique to an individual, enduring over time, and a consequence of human experiences. Middle leadership is often the first promotion for teachers from teacher to leader and, as such, how middle leaders perceive themselves as a leader and how this formative process of leadership identity underpins middle leaders' practices can make a significant impact on a leader's decision making, professional relationships, behaviours, and actions. This chapter is co-authored by two researchers and two middle leaders with the intention of understanding middle leader identity development and its influence on middle leadership practices. Using interviews, middle leaders' stories of identity were co-composed and re-storied to construct each middle leader's narrative. This chapter concludes with a discussion on the influences of identity for middle leaders and considerations for leadership development.

Keywords: Middle leadership; school leadership; leadership identity; self-awareness; leader development; narrative

GUIDING QUESTIONS

The following are questions that you should ask yourself before you commence reading this chapter. The questions ask you to consider what you already know and feel about the topic.

1. How would you describe your leadership?
2. What are some key influences that have shaped how you lead?
3. What are the strengths in the way you lead? How do you know they are strengths? What is the outcome?
4. What areas could you further develop in the way you lead? What are the possible positive outcomes?

INTRODUCTION

A school leader's identity includes their beliefs on school leadership, the extent to which they perceive they embody this, and how important their school leadership identity is within their overall personal identity (Lord & Hall, 2005). It combines aspects of a school leader's personal and social identities and is influenced by the individual's unique personal characteristics (e.g. values, beliefs, and motivations) and their personal, social, and relational experiences (e.g. previous experiences of being led or leading). A school leader's identity is demonstrated through their repeated actions, behaviours, and practices. The construction of one's leadership identity is a social and relational process (Ely et al., 2011; Shollen, 2018) that occurs through reflecting, internalising, and defining leadership in reference to one's school context, relationships, and perceptions of self (Epitropaki et al., 2017). Leadership identity takes time to construct, is dynamic, and evolves as a school leader reflects, adapts, and grows based on their experiences, challenges, and relationships (Cruz-González et al., 2021). In their systematic review of principal leadership identity, Cruz-González et al. (2021) found that identity formation is facilitated through school leaders' professional learning specifically in educational leadership, combined with supported critical leadership experiences. A strong school leadership identity has been found to be important for school improvement, specifically in creating and motivating teams, gaining colleague commitment, and building shared vision (Ritacco & Bolivar, 2018).

Leadership identity is important for all levels of school leadership; however, for middle leaders, identity is especially significant and complex. Middle leaders are formally appointed leaders, with accountable responsibilities, who operate between senior leaders and teachers, and lead to positively impact teaching and student learning (Lipscombe et al., 2021). This often requires middle leaders to balance the competing demands and interests of their classroom teacher colleagues and school executives. This is particularly challenging for middle leaders, first because their middle leadership role is often their first promotion from teacher to leader, and second, in Australia, there is a lack of clarity around middle leader roles, responsibilities, and practices (Lipscombe et al., 2020). The dual role of working as and between teachers and leaders creates challenges for leadership identity. Middle leaders already have a professional identity as a teacher before coming into middle leadership. While research is limited in the field specific to leadership identity and school middle leadership, research associated with middle leadership more broadly argues that middle leaders create new identities as leaders and may face challenges with their new leadership identity as their teaching and leadership identities collide (McGivern et al., 2015). This complexity and the acknowledged lack of specific middle leader professional learning (Gurr & Drysdale, 2013) has implications for how school middle leaders purposefully construct their leadership identity. This chapter explores two school middle leaders' construction of their middle leadership identity, how it is developed (or not), and the implications this has for their middle leadership practices.

RESEARCH DESIGN

This chapter draws on data from a larger scaled study aimed at exploring middle leaders' leadership identity. Emma and Sam, who participated in the larger study, have co-authored this paper with two researchers. For this chapter, data were collected through interviews. The interviews represent 'biographical narratives' (Black et al., 2010) of Emma and Sam's middle leadership from their responses to interview questions posed by the researchers. The aim of the interviews was to gain a sense of how middle leaders in the same leadership program perceive and practice their own leadership identity. Interviews were conducted online via Zoom, were recorded, and then transcribed.

After transcription, the two researchers 're-storied' Emma and Sam's interview responses to construct a coherent narrative of their leadership identity. This analytical process involved a thematic approach whereby themes were drawn out of the interviews in a way that retained the story in its entirety (Riessman, 2008). At the compilation of this analytical step, Emma, and Sam as co-researchers, checked if the re-storied narratives were correct representations of their experiences and added further meaning and detail if required. Five factors were found to surface in Emma and Sam's leadership identity: relational leadership, support from others, credibility, positionality, and self – and social awareness. Emma and Sam, as co-composers of meaning, reflected on these themes to provide further insights into each factor.

FINDINGS

Meet Emma and Sam

In this section, Emma and Sam will introduce themselves as middle leaders including their past and former experiences and settings.

Emma

I am a middle-aged middle leader who has worked across the Western Australian public primary school sector since graduating from university in 2006. My professional experience spans a broad range of contexts. My early teaching career was predominantly situated in a high socioeconomic metropolitan area. I then worked in two low socioeconomic schools and while on maternity leave, I lived in a remote Aboriginal community where my children attended the playgroup at the local remote community school. Currently, I have established myself in a remote public school as a middle leader in the role of acting Deputy Principal and Curriculum Leader. The collective experience of working and being part of a range of school communities has had a positive influence on my professional identity, particularly in developing my interpersonal acumen. Collectively, these experiences have taught me to build trust, model cultural competencies, and naturally develop a rapport with people from all walks of life, which I know creates the conditions for leading strong partnerships and collaboration.

Sam

I am a middle-aged male and have been in education full-time since 2014. Prior to my first full-time appointment as a teacher, I worked in the private sector holding a variety of roles in leadership, management, and Indigenous health and well-being. This broadened my real-life experiences and provided leadership opportunities that have helped shape who I am and how I now lead in schools. During my teaching career, I have taught across primary schools, remote community schools, and senior high schools in Western Australia. I have held various middle leadership positions including curriculum leader, Year Leader, and Program Coordinator in Behaviour Management. I also recently held acting Principal positions in two remote community schools.

CO-CONSTRUCTED MIDDLE LEADERSHIP IDENTITY

In this section, the researchers and middle leaders co-constructed an understanding of middle leadership identity. First, the researchers present re-storied identities of Emma and Sam. These identities are the product of the narrative analysis of interview data by the researchers. The re-storied identities are followed by personal reflections in first person by Emma and Sam.

Emma's Re-storied Identity

Emma describes her middle leadership identity as being 'genuine', 'strategic', and 'pragmatic'. She explained that she has good interpersonal and communication skills which makes her 'approachable' so that her peers can be 'comfortable talking' to her. She believes that as a middle leader, building 'good morale', learning alongside her colleagues as opposed to leading from the 'top-down', leading change, and 'getting things done' are important parts of how she and others see her as a middle leader. As a result of the enormity of her role leading numeracy and literacy, she identifies that being 'strategic' and 'pragmatic' is an important aspect of her practice and the school in which she works must have a strong identity and clear 'structures, routines, and processes' to enable her to lead effectively. Emma disclosed that at times she does suffer from 'imposter syndrome' and finds having 'difficult conversations' with people challenging as she is a 'people pleaser'.

Emma's greatest influence on her middle leadership identity are her mum and a former principal. Her mum was her 'coach' and helped her gain confidence and clarity with her career pathway. Her former principal invested in her leadership development and who Emma identified as a positive role model for seeing 'the big picture' and 'developing his staff'.

From an analysis of Emma's identity from the interview, it appears that Emma's identity is shaped by three key areas: relational leadership, the support she receives from others, and her credibility in curriculum.

EMMA'S PERSONAL REFLECTION ON HER MIDDLE LEADERSHIP IDENTITY

In this section, Emma reflects on the areas that have shaped her middle leadership identity with the intention of reporting on how and why these three areas shape her identity and consequent practices as a middle leader.

Relational Leadership: Being Prepared and Positive

The quality of my day-to-day interactions is crucial for the success of my role. In my previous position as a classroom teacher, my primary focus was building relationships with the students in my class. However, as a middle leader, my attention has shifted towards fostering strong connections with the teachers in my school. I love working with students across my school, but it is the nature of the relationship with their teachers that is pivotal to my role. Developing a rapport, building trust, communicating a vision, setting goals, addressing problems, and leading change are all part of my relational leadership. However, as a person who identifies as a people pleaser, who avoids conflict, and who wants to be liked, working in the capacity of a middle leader has really challenged me. I am building my confidence in this space by taking the time to rehearse effective, open-ended coaching questions to build my own capacity.

Knowing and understanding the classrooms, even though I am now not a classroom teacher, is important to the way I lead. As a classroom teacher, I appreciated seeing members of the school leadership team touch base with me in my classroom on a regular basis, so I try hard to do the rounds in classrooms most mornings. It might sound simple, but it is hard to talk about school vision, classroom teaching and learning, or even students, when you don't have a good handle on what's happening in classrooms or have a rapport with the students. Prioritising time in classrooms in the morning builds collegiality because I can acknowledge my teacher colleagues' work in the context of their work, providing specific and timely feedback. As well, morning visits often allow teachers to quickly troubleshoot problems with me, saving them time and an email.

When visiting classrooms in the morning, I take photos of great things I see (e.g. of a teacher developed resource). I routinely use images from around my school in our fortnightly staff meetings and school development days. It has been an impactful strategy because it is celebrating our school community and subtly (and strategically) communicates to school staff what exemplary practice looks like. Beginning meetings in this way, especially when they can be overrun by administrative and operational agendas, sets a tone that is student-focused and positive.

Other strategies I utilise to build meaningful relationships with colleagues include acknowledging others and their contributions by writing appreciation notes and placing them in my colleague's pigeonhole or purchasing takeaway coffee and leaving it on my colleague's desk in the morning.

Support From Others

I have several people in my network who have been transformational in their support of me as a leader. My mum has had the most significant influence on my career and leadership journey. She is a qualified secondary English teacher, but her career ultimately led her to work (and lead) outside of education, with children still at the core of her work. My mum as my coach helped me to articulate my strengths and the broad and overarching skills that I bring to my role. For example, effective time management, ability to prioritise, and showing a level of empathy to others. This has influenced how I conceptualise school leadership, that leadership attributes and broader competencies trump expert or specialised curriculum knowledge alone. As a critical friend who knows me very well, my mum has been a sounding board when talking through a problem and has modelled big picture strategic thinking.

I have worked under five different principals, but my previous school principal was the most influential to my leadership identity. I was a classroom teacher when he began at the school, and over time, he developed processes so that teachers, including myself, who aspired to leadership, were identified and professionally developed through mentoring and goal setting. As part of this leadership identification and support, I completed a 360-degree feedback survey which utilised self-assessment and colleague feedback to identify thinking, behavioural styles, and effectiveness. My previous principal continues to invest in my leadership journey by touching base regularly and recommending literature to read.

Credibility in the Curriculum – Co-learner and Expert

Credibility is very important to me as a middle leader. I think credibility is something that is built over time but can erode quickly.

Thinking about it in this way, credibility is then also something that needs to be maintained.

Across my middle leadership experience, transitioning to new roles and in new schools were important spaces for me to build credibility. A successful strategy I employed was to develop and distribute a needs analysis to all teaching staff. For example, as a Numeracy Curriculum Leader, I was allocated two days per week to my middle leadership role. I needed to be strategic and organised with my time to make the most of those two days. The needs analysis took the form of a survey with a series of questions regarding what teachers identified was lacking in the school's Mathematics program, the resources they used to teach Mathematics, and their perceived strengths and weaknesses in teaching. Employing a needs analysis provided a large volume of qualitative data which informed my decision making and confirmed the direction I needed to go regarding leading mathematics teaching and learning at the school. Feedback from the needs analysis allowed me to implement some big changes in a relatively short period of time because I was able to quickly identify what needed to happen first. Importantly, inviting teachers to put a voice in the direction of the school meant they had buy-in and greater ownership of the implementation process.

SAM'S RE-STORIED IDENTITY

Sam describes his middle leadership identity as a 'connection between school leadership, teachers and students'. Sam explains that as a middle leader, he focuses on the 'nuts and bolts' of 'curriculum delivery' while also supporting the 'operational and strategic' directions of the school.

Professional relationships are the most significant aspect of Sam's leadership identity in terms of the relationships he forms with students, staff, the leadership team, as well as the regional leadership team in which the school is situated. Sam explained that while relationships are important, he knows that 'disagreement or conflict' is part of his role, and consequently, he focuses on building high 'levels of trust and respect' and utilises strategies such as professional and planned conversations focused on teaching and learning that enable him to surface differences of opinions with the teachers he leads while ensuring things are 'heading in the right direction'.

Sam identified that having a strong sense of self was important to his leadership identity. 'Knowing who you are, and how you might respond in certain situations or being able to draw upon experiences where you've been challenged' is important for Sam to provide transparent and consistent leadership when leading others.

From an analysis of Sam's identity from the interview, it appears that Sam's identity is shaped by three key areas: relational leadership based on trust, his positionality as a middle leader, and his awareness of self and others.

SAM'S PERSONAL REFLECTION ON HIS MIDDLE LEADERSHIP IDENTITY

In this section, Sam considers what shapes his identity with the intention of reporting on how and why three key aspects are significant and consequently are practised as a middle leader.

Relational Leadership: Building Trust But Not Shying Away From Conflict

I believe it is critical to build trust with colleagues. I do this by being true to who I am. I am laid back and easy-going, enjoy peace and harmony, and bringing people together. I enjoy the responsibility that comes with leadership; it helps me be the best version of myself. Although my default way of working with others is in a calm and non-conflicting approach, I am committed to ensuring my actions match my words even when facing challenging situations. I know that this can create tension or conflict at times, particularly when my values are challenged, but I approach this by finding common ground with those who have different perspectives and ensuring together we agree on the next best step to move forward. I have found that developing a personal connection, discovering who a teacher is beyond the school gate and interacting with them on a personal level, is useful when building positive relationships with colleagues.

Being a parent has helped provide me with a better perspective of relationships in delicate situations and has added a greater dimension to my leadership. Parenthood has helped me with situations requiring contact with parents, having empathy for them, and being able to relate to their emotions and seek the best outcome for all concerned, the student, the parent, and the staff member. Also, leading and working with teaching staff who are parents is an important connection for me and how I lead. The connection we share together centres around navigating the challenges of family life with the complexities of being an educator. Having this common ground helps build relational trust and empathy.

Positionality: Between Classroom, Teachers, and Leadership

I am a member of the school leadership team which includes program coordinators, curriculum leaders, deputies, and the principal. I hold a unique position within the school, with no teaching role. I traverse between classroom support for students and staff by diagnosing student behaviours that impact student learning and achievement. This position also requires providing information to, and making decisions with, administration teams and heads of learning areas to shape the direction of the school when providing resource allocation to address student behaviour and staff professional development.

Unlike other middle leaders, I don't manage staff, and I don't conduct performance management with colleagues, but I do hold a formal leadership position in the school and report to the Deputy Principal. This positionality, working with teachers but not being formally responsible for their performance, can be challenging, especially when needing to address a concern. A strategy I use to combat this challenge is offering observation, coaching, and feedback to staff. These strategies help me as a middle leader bridge the gap between the classroom and the executive. I can offer insights into what is happening in the classroom, from both the student and staff perspective, and participate in dialogue with the school's senior leadership team about addressing issues.

One of my current challenges with positionality is my past experiences as a principal. In my current school, I am a middle leader but have had secondments as a principal in two other schools. Leading a whole school, I have learned and developed strategic thinking and understand its importance to professional conversations, decision making, and school improvement. On returning to my school as a middle leader, my challenge is to be valued for my prior experience to support the strategic and operational needs of the school.

Self and Social Awareness (Relationship Between Knowing Oneself and the Impact This Has on Others)

Understanding and reflecting on who I am, what my unconscious bias is, knowing what triggers my negative and unproductive behaviours, and what conditions are needed to ensure I am at my best (positive and productive), all help to shape the type of leader I am. I believe I need to focus on the best version of myself, in order to be at my best when leading others.

Through practising gratitude and mindfulness, journal writing, and regular reflection, I dissect situations and conversations that have had both positive and negative outcomes, with the purpose of making changes in future scenarios to ensure the best possible outcomes. I seek regular feedback, from trusted colleagues, to provide an alternative perspective as an important tool to help shape myself and social awareness. I also plan, draft, and rehearse scripts to prevent my behaviours from negatively impacting myself and others and so that my best self can be present in all exchanges. One useful strategy I have engaged with is a survey titled 'The Print Survey from the Paul Hertz Group', aimed at proving feedback on why you do what you do, say what you say, and think what you think. This survey helped me to discover more about my why and my purpose. I regularly reflect on the information this survey has uncovered about me and draw upon what I need to do to prepare my best self in various situations.

DISCUSSION

The findings from this study suggest that leadership identity is significant, formative, and a catalyst to middle leaders' relationships, beliefs, and practices. The findings align with previous research on school leaders' identity which suggested a strong school leader identity is an antecedent for effective leading practices (Cruz-González et al., 2021) and central to positive relationships (Mpungose, 2010).

This study revealed Emma and Sam's evolving leadership identity is very much a social construct, where their own identity is often referenced in relation to others including colleagues and family. This is no surprise given research literature into leadership identity often relates identity with a social identity approach, where leaders derive a sense of self not only from what makes them unique and special as individuals but also from their membership in a social group and their commonalities with other group members (Hogg & Terry, 2000). Socialisation experiences were foundational to Emma and Sam's middle leadership identity which included authority figures (e.g. mother, past principal), personal experiences (e.g. parent), and professional experiences (e.g. as teacher, principal). Previous studies have highlighted the complex interplay of both personal and professional experiences in the construction of a school leader's identity (Cruz-González et al., 2021).

Leading requires more than the acquisition of a position, instead it is often a transformational shift that comes with uncertainty and discomfort. Research that explores identity and middle leadership suggest that leaders must develop a clear leadership identity that does not compromise their professional (e.g. teacher) or personal identity (McGivern et al., 2015; Spehar et al., 2015). Emma identified her leadership identity was at times entangled in challenges associated with leading others which resulted in her feeling like an 'imposter', and as such, she found it challenging to have difficult conversations with colleagues. Sam shared that his personal identity as a parent was an enabler to his leadership. Conversely, his unusual transition from middle leader, to acting principal, and then back to middle leader has resulted in a feeling that his experience is not always valued or utilised to its full extent, showing that politics and context impact construction of professional identity (Cruz-González et al., 2021). These examples highlight the significance of leadership identity as not only evolving based on time, space, and experience but also the difficulties of navigating personal, professional, and leadership identities.

It was clear that both middle leaders were identified as both a teacher and a leader and as a result led between two subcultures of teachers and leaders (Lipscombe et al., 2021). Language such as 'working alongside', 'connections between senior leaders and teachers', and 'bridging the gap' permeated Emma and Sam's descriptions of their leadership identity, indicating the significance of middle leaders staying in the middle and working strategically as a key broker between teachers and senior leaders. The dual nature of teacher and leader identity was not without its challenges (e.g. not be recognised for expertise, lack of confidence to tackle conflict); however, both middle leaders strategically implemented strategies to understand and develop themselves as a leader while also paying close attention to positive relationships with others. Table 1.1 overviews the range of strategies both middle leaders enacted to navigate their identity as teacher and leader.

Table 1.1. Strategies to Lead Self and Others.

	Strategies
Knowing and developing self as a leader	• Peer feedback • Development of conversation scripts • Rehearsal of conversations prior to implementing • Surveys • Journaling • Practising gratitude and mindfulness
Knowing and developing others	• Visiting classrooms each morning • Taking photos of practice to share and celebrate at staff meetings • Writing appreciation notes to colleagues • Purchasing coffee for colleagues • Developing a personal connection with colleagues beyond their role in school • Offering optional observations, coaching, and feedback to staff • Completing a needs analysis of colleagues' needs and wants

Source: Authors' own creation.

CONCLUSION

Supporting middle leaders to continuously explore and develop their leadership identity is an important aspect of leadership development. The re-storied narratives of Emma and Sam, and their associated reflections, suggest that leadership identity is not only an important aspect of understanding how middle leadership is practised but that a deliberate focus on leadership identity is a powerful source for continued growth as a middle leader. Importantly, from a methodological perspective, middle leaders working with researchers was a powerful learning opportunity to learn together through research and practice. We encourage future scholars and middle leaders to elaborate on our findings by designing studies that can shed further insights on middle leadership identity.

REFLECTIVE QUESTIONS

Now that you have read Emma and Sam's story, take some time to reflect on your leadership identity and how it has developed.

1. How would you describe your leadership?
2. What are some key influences that have shaped how you lead?
3. What are the strengths in the way you lead? How do you know they are strengths? What is the outcome?
4. What areas could you further develop in the way you lead? What are the possible positive outcomes?

REFERENCES

Black, L., Williams, J., Hernandez-Martinez, P., Davis, P., Pampaka, M., & Wake, G. (2010). Developing a 'leading identity': The relationship between students' mathematical identities and their career and higher education aspirations. *Educational Studies in Mathematics*, *73*(1), 55–72.

Cruz-González, C., Rodríguez, C. L., & Segovia, J. D. (2021). A systematic review of principals' leadership identity from 1993 to 2019. *Educational Management Administration & Leadership*, *49*(1), 31–53.

Ely, R. J., Ibarra, H., & Kolb, D. (2011). Taking gender into account: Theory and design for women's leadership development programs. *Academy of Management Learning and Education*, *10*, 374–393.

Epitropaki, O., Kark, R., Mainemelis, C., & Lord, R. G. (2017). Leadership and followership identity processes: A multilevel review. *Leadership Quarterly*, *28*(1), 104–129.

Gurr, D., & Drysdale, L. (2013). Middle-level secondary school leaders: Potential, constraints and implications for leadership preparation and development. *Journal of Educational Administration*, *51*(1), 55–71.

Hogg, M. A., & Terry, D. J. (2000). Social identity and self-categorization processes in organizational contexts. *Academy of Management Review*, *25*, 121–140.

Lipscombe, K., Grice, C., Tindall-Ford, S., & De-Nobile, J. (2020). Middle leading in Australian schools: Professional standards, positions, and professional development. *School Leadership & Management*, *40*(5), 406–424.

Lipscombe, K., Tindall-Ford, S., & Lamanna, J. (2021). School middle leadership: A systematic review. *Educational Management Administration and Leadership*, *19*(1), 1–19.

Lord, R. G., & Hall, R. J. (2005). Identity, deep structure and the development of leadership skill. *The Leadership Quarterly*, *16*(4), 591–615.

McGivern, G., Currie, G., Ferlie, E., Fitzgerald, L., & Waring, J. (2015). Hybrid manager-professionals' identity work: The maintenance and hybridization of medical professionalism in managerial contexts. *Public Administration*, *93*(2), 412–432

Mpungose, J. (2010). Constructing principals' professional identities through life stories: An exploration. *South African Journal of Education*, *30*, 527–537.

Riessman, C. K. (2008). *Narrative methods for the human sciences*. Sage Publications, Inc.

Ritacco, M., & Bolívar, A. (2018). School principals in Spain: An unstable identity. *International Journal of Educational Leadership and Management*, *6*(1), 18–39.

Shollen, S. L. (2018). Women's leader identity development: Building a team for the journey'. In S. J. Tan & L. DeFrank-Cole (Eds.), *Women's leadership journeys: Stories, research and novel perspectives* (pp. 162–177). Routledge.

Spehar, I., Frich, J. C., & Kjekshus, L. E. (2015). Professional identity and role transitions in clinical managers. *Journal of Health Organization and Management*, *29*(3), 353–366.

2

LEARNING ABOUT AND LEADING FROM THE MIDDLE: STORIES FROM THREE WOMEN MIDDLE LEADERS

Danielle Cioffi[a], Nichole Tiller[a], Lucy Warnock[b] and Barbara Watterston[c]

[a]*Cedar College, Northgate, SA, Australia*
[b]*Immanuel College, Novar Gardens, SA, Australia*
[c]*Australian Council for Educational Leaders, Melbourne, Victoria, Australia*

ABSTRACT

The focus of this chapter lies with women middle-level leaders. It reports on themes from women in leadership programmes designed and delivered by Barbara Watterston, through the lens of a programme especially developed for the Association of Independent Schools of South Australia (AISSA). This chapter begins by profiling a description of the programme. The main aim was providing women leaders with an opportunity to take stock of their careers, consider ongoing challenges impeding their work as school leaders, and identify options for the future. After the programme finished, volunteers were invited to write a narrative encapsulating their career journey. Three women leaders volunteered, and their insightful reflections regarding their career trajectories constitute a significant portion of this chapter. The final part of this chapter identifies three common themes that emerged from their stories, resonating with ideas which are frequently illuminated in similar programmes and research. These include the importance of ongoing professional learning to be a successful leader, gender-based barriers that caused the women to doubt their abilities and readiness for leadership, and the deep appreciation the women expressed from learning with and from like-minded other women leaders.

Keywords: Middle leader; mentoring; gender; women in leadership programme; narratives; empowerment

GUIDING QUESTIONS

The following are questions that you should ask yourself before you commence reading this chapter. The questions ask you to consider what you already know and feel about the topic.

1. How do you conceptualise middle leadership: is it a steppingstone to senior leadership OR is it a fulfilling role in itself?
2. What are gender-based barriers that can limit women's decision to pursue leadership roles?
3. Where am I in my career and what is the next step?

INTRODUCTION

The themes of and chapters in this book are concerned with middle leaders in schools and the challenges they face in their work. Middle leadership is a unique form of leadership in schools. Middle leaders are leaders who exist at the interface between senior leaders and teachers. Like other leaders, they are formally appointed and hold accountabilities for their important work that is often concerned with instructional leadership (Lipscombe et al., 2021).

Because of their location in the 'middle', middle leaders face unique tensions or polarities. According to Johnson (Kise, 2023a), polarities are sets of values that are interdependent; neither set works without consideration from the other (Kise, 2023a). Some of the polarities for middle leadership suggest that middle leaders are both teachers and leaders, leaders and colleagues, and leaders and learners. To see a middle leader as a 'leader' and not as a 'teacher' reveals only part of the story as 'both/and thinking is an essential addition to either/or thinking' (Johnson, 2020, in Kise, 2023b, p. 12). The value of 'and' rather than 'or' positions the middle leader as a person who juggles multiple responsibilities and roles when leading in and from the middle.

This chapter celebrates middle school leadership and middle leaders. It begins by providing a description of a leadership programme that I co-designed and delivered for women middle leaders. Following this are stories from the field which include narratives written by three women middle leaders who participated in the programme. Each of them provides insightful reflections regarding their career journeys, their struggles, as well as their triumphs as middle leaders, and where they are at now in their respective careers. The final part of this chapter identifies some themes that emerged from the women's narratives.

WOMEN IN LEADERSHIP PROGRAMME

I have had the privilege of crafting, co-constructing, and delivering many women in leadership programmes nationally and internationally. For the purposes of this chapter, we have distilled insights gathered through the lens of the *Women in Leadership* programme especially developed for Association of Independent Schools of South Australia (AISSA) and targeted women middle-level leaders. Its aim was to provide an opportunity for women middle leaders to take stock of their career journey to date and to consider the challenges, ongoing opportunities, and options they continue to face in their work as leaders. Anecdotally, there is a sense that there is a need for a more strategic and intentional focus on leadership aspirations or ambition among women educators, yet the research suggests that there is a myriad of gender-based barriers impacting women aspiring to leadership. Another aim of the programme, then, was to provide an opportunity for the women middle leaders to connect with and learn from other successful women, from both inside and outside of education, share experiences and effective practices, including lessons learned and strategies for encouraging other women into leadership, and build motivation for and confidence in their work as leaders. As described in conversations with AISSA Director, Mary Hudson, it was important to co-design a beautifully structured and challenging programme to address these issues through tailored professional learning focused on personal and professional growth for women. Over the spaced three-day programme, participants were asked to reflect on why a focus on women in leadership is so important, how to step into their power and craft their own leadership identity, and how to make a short presentation that enabled them to share their professional learnings to date. A highlight of the programme was the opportunity to connect with a professional companion, an experienced woman leader, who provided the space for open dialogue where doubts, challenges, gender barriers and complexities, self-imposed limitations, and ambitions could be openly shared.

More recent programmes, including AISSA's, have been based around my co-authored book with Jane Kise, *Step in, Step Up* (Kise &Watterston, 2019), which provides practical strategies and support for women aspiring to leadership roles, including a comprehensive discussion of the literature on gender stereotypes that limit both genders. Previously, as a teacher, in formal and informal leader roles, the voices and themes shared below, the doubts, the challenges, and the '*ah ah*' moments are all reminiscent of my own which guided me into research focused not only on women and leadership but also on championing school leadership development and more broadly targeted and personalised professional learning. Women in the programme were given opportunities to consider these barriers and the extent to which they resonated with their own leadership struggles and directions.

STORIES FROM THE FIELD

After the *Women in Leadership* programme concluded, volunteers were sought to write a narrative encapsulating their leadership journey that has led them to their current middle leadership role.

Participants were also asked to share insights regarding lessons they were able to distil from the leadership programme in which they participated. Three participants volunteered, and their stories are given below.

As you read Danielle, Lucy, and Nichole's stories, reflect on the connections to your middle leadership experience. What resonates with you? What about their leadership experiences affirms your leadership story and what provokes you to rethink your own experiences? What challenges have they overcome? What supportive structures have helped them work through the challenges of leading from the middle?

Danielle Cioffi

When I first began my teaching career at 22, I didn't think about the future. I just knew that I loved teaching and working with students. I figured that I'd probably remain in the classroom for an extended period – perhaps for the entirety of my career. Career progression wasn't anywhere in my mind. In my first couple of years working as a teacher, I began to understand how little I knew about pedagogy and learning. I knew what worked in a classroom from my experience, but I was desperately curious to know *why*. I returned to university and earned my master's degree in education with a focus on gifted education. As I completed my formal study, and engaged with as much professional development as I could, I found that my role within the school changed. I was presenting more workshops to staff and proposing curriculum changes to the leadership team. During my 20s, I ended up holding a year-level coordinator position for six years and started our high school's gifted education programme. I had not planned either of these leadership opportunities, but they blossomed from my interests and study.

Very recently, I was appointed to the position of Director of High School Curriculum. The journey to get from where I started to where I am now has taken some time. Yet, I nearly didn't apply for this position as I felt it was perhaps, 'too soon' or 'too early' in my career, and that perhaps I should wait until I was older and more experienced. I was initially concerned that there was a risk that either colleagues or parents may not take me seriously or respect my authority to make decisions, due to my age. This is an issue that I have experienced before, in less-senior leadership roles. I also had the fear that someone else could do the job 'better' than me, but I have since learned to trust that I have been appointed to my leadership positions for a reason, and that there is no shame in growing and developing as you move into a role. It's not possible to know everything, and what a relief it is to know this!

There is no doubt that my self-confidence has grown slowly over my career, as I have learned new skills, engaged in different forms of professional development, and felt more comfortable and capable in the classroom. This, in conjunction with the support of my colleagues, has helped me reach a point where I finally feel that my skills and knowledge are at a level where I can not only manage my new position but also make a positive impact within it. I am enjoying thoroughly my new role as Director of High School Curriculum, and it has been an important time of challenge and growth for me.

At this point in my career, I feel as if I have reached the kind of leadership role that suits my personality and skillset. Yet, I do wonder what will come next as I look forward to a career in education until my retirement. It seems that in society, success is equated with moving up the ladder, so what happens when you don't want to go any further? I have no interest in pursuing more senior titles for the sake of 'progressing'. I will be better served by formulating my own ideas of what career success looks like – whether it's further study, a new role, or perhaps even returning to the classroom full-time down the track.

When considering where I want my career to go from here, I think the most satisfying answer I can articulate is that I simply want to be in a position where I am making a positive impact on students – whether that is in leadership, in a classroom, or both. Leadership is about more than titles. We can all be leaders in our classrooms and our own contexts. I am looking forward to my new role as a chance to learn and develop and to be able to support my colleagues in doing so too. We all win (teachers, leaders, and students) when we share learning and growth opportunities. To be able to put aside my perfectionism and the high standards that I imposed upon myself is a significant mental barrier that has been lifted and has made my transition into leadership a much easier one. I am very grateful to the work of the AISSA, and the leadership programme run by Dr Barbara Watterson, who made me aware of how gender-based barriers work to limit women's careers and career choices. It has been incredibly empowering to be reminded that none of us is alone in our work or our leadership journeys. Supportive networks are vital for all teachers to ensure that we can learn and develop for the sake of our students and ourselves.

Lucy Warnock

'We all win if we lift women'. The moment I heard Barb Watterston speak these words, I had an instant connection. What I didn't know was that the *Women in Leadership* programme was going to be the most empowering development opportunity I have been a part of in my professional career. It came at the perfect time.

I have been a middle leader from the early stage of my teaching career. By the time I was 30, I had been a year-level coordinator, a faculty leader, and at 29, I was appointed as Assistant Principal in an acting capacity. After four years of parental leave, I returned to teaching part-time and within two years, I was back in middle leadership. I am still working in that capacity 14 years later. Although I have used the word 'still', it is not with negative emotion. It was never my intention to move into leadership so quickly after parental leave. It is not what I had planned. My leaders identified a skillset, and as it was a middle leadership position, I convinced myself that it was an opportunity that I could not pass. It allowed me to be in the classroom and do what I loved, teaching students, but it also allowed me to dip my toe back in the water in terms of leadership. Even though I have been successful over this time, my personal struggle of being 100% present as a leader, classroom teacher, and parent, is something I reflect on often.

For a long time, I have been my biggest critic, and this has held me back from taking risks primarily due to the dreaded 'imposter syndrome'. Fear of judgement, not having all the skills, valuing my family before work, and playing safe are all factors that have interfered. As a middle leader, I play safe. I know that I have the skillset and the capacity to lead beyond, but the thought of aspiring to that next level is where I doubt myself, and it is easier to stay in my comfort zone where I feel that I am in control.

On starting the *Women Leadership* programme, I knew that leadership was something I wanted to pursue. I have had my 'eye on that prize' at our school for a long time. I have acted in the position on many occasions and have done so successfully, but I believed that middle leadership was the only leadership position I was capable of. So many doubting questions have plagued me:

> *There is no way that I would be able to do this at another school. What if the next school I work at doesn't see my leadership skills like my present workplace does? What if I am not valued because I have not furthered my studies and I only have experience to rely on? Moreover, if had a senior leadership position, would I struggle by not being in the classroom?*

Being part of the *Women in Leadership* programme has empowered me to look for many different opportunities. Connected by a group of women who shared similar experiences gave me the confidence to acknowledge my strengths in a public forum. The relationships were liberating and many of us found the confidence to start believing in our capabilities and challenging the dreaded imposter syndrome. The connection with an external mentor also forced me to articulate my strengths, and it was the first time that I had started to think about leadership in a strategic manner. I am starting networking and making connections with other leaders nationwide. My new role as Wellbeing Coordinator has given me the scope and capacity to do this.

Right now, I am where I want to be. I have been blessed with amazing leaders at my current site who have always encouraged and empowered me. I am being supported in my growth but need to remind myself that by staying here, it is my choice, and that I am not doing it for others. Loyalty is an exceptional quality to have, but it can also be one that limits your opportunities, especially when you are leading from the middle. I have learnt that being loyal also means being loyal to myself and ensuring that I make decisions with that in mind too.

On the final day of the *Women in Leadership* programme, we were asked to share an artefact that represented our thinking and experience. A colleague once gave me a pair of wise owls and I chose them as my artefact. A female colleague who joined my team in 2015, who is now a very dear friend, was one of the first women who recognised and celebrated my abilities as a leader. When her tenure was up, I gave her one of the owls as a parting gift in hope that one day we would work together again, and the owls would be reunited. She gave me the confidence to acknowledge my strengths and was the very reason why I started to believe in myself as a leader. By lifting me, I have been able to lift others and together we have created many winners.

Nichole Tiller

When I began my middle management leadership journey six years ago, I stepped into a level of leadership I had never experienced before and in a new school. Not surprisingly, I felt as though I had been thrown in the deep end. Not only did I need to learn and develop new leadership skills, but I also had to learn about the policies, procedures, culture, and people in my new school. I felt overwhelmed and very alone. I was the only female on the leadership team and despite the supportive and welcoming male leaders, I was craving a female role model. I did not know whom to ask or how to find a woman leader who could mentor me. I was acutely conscious of the weight of not wanting to disappoint anyone or not meet the expectations of staff, especially the female staff. Being new to the role and middle management, I lacked confidence in my ability as a leader, often feeling under-qualified, under-skilled, and not competent enough to maintain the position. I also did not feel I had anyone I could share my feelings with as I didn't want anyone else to think I wasn't coping in the role.

My feelings of inadequacy were reinforced by feedback I received from staff based on a leadership survey. This survey is conducted on all middle and senior leaders in every three areas to provide them with valuable feedback on their leadership and reveal areas of strength and growth. The feedback I received suggested that I was perceived as not confident as a leader. It was at this point that I decided I could either admit defeat and look for a non-leadership role or I could do something about upskilling myself to improve and be a better leader. After processing the information and talking with my husband, I realised that I had been a bit too hard on myself given it was only early days in a new role, in a new school where I was still developing myself as a leader and establishing relationships.

Working out what to do with the feedback and how to use it to improve my skills was empowering as I was able to choose the next step in my leadership journey. The feedback no longer had a hold over me; instead, I used it as the drive I needed to move forward. I decided to enrol in a Master of Education (with a leadership focus). I knew it was a big commitment but felt the timing was right, so I took a leap of faith and applied. This was a pivotal moment in my leadership journey. Study provided opportunities for me to learn about different leadership styles, enabling me to identify my own style, how to lead effectively, providing examples and strategies of how to lead well, and issues women in leadership face.

During the *Women in Leadership* programme, I experienced two significant 'ah ha' moments. The first occurred when Barb shared statements made by Georgie Harman (CEO of Beyond Blue) regarding 'vulnerability'. She declared *vulnerability is your superpower, lean into it and do not be afraid to share your vulnerability; it has a ripple effect.* All this time, I had been fighting to do/be the opposite. I did not want anyone to see my vulnerability as I feared they would think I was incompetent and not suitable for leadership and consequently my role. Yet, I came to appreciate that being vulnerable could make me more relatable, approachable, and trustworthy as a leader.

My second 'ah ha' moment, closely linked to my first, occurred when Barb introduced the concept of the 'imposter syndrome'. I had not heard of this concept previously, but as soon as we started unpacking it, I could relate instantaneously to its meaning. Minimising my own success, comparing myself to others, focusing too much on being perfect, and dialling down my own ambition for fear of being exposed were key characteristics of this syndrome. They were the exact attitudes I had been struggling with. I had felt inadequate to do my role, I did not celebrate the wins I had achieved. I focused on the areas I had failed and not on my successes. I looked at other leaders, comparing my own abilities to theirs, instead of celebrating the differences in our giftings and strengths and how they help us to be better. Learning about this was like lifting a heavy weight from my shoulders. I felt validated, encouraged, and no longer alone.

I have now completed both the Master of Education degree and the *Women in Leadership* programme. I feel empowered to be vulnerable, to work to my strengths, and not be afraid of the areas I need to improve in. I am inspired by stories other women in leadership have shared regarding their journey, and I feel passionate about being a woman in leadership who encourages and supports other women to step up and not be afraid to give leadership a go.

SOME FINAL THOUGHTS AND REFLECTIONS

There are several themes common to Lucy, Nichole, and Danielle's middle leader journey. First is the *importance of ongoing professional learning* if one is going to be successful as a leader in schools today. Professional development in middle leadership is often left to chance. The stories and feedback from the many leadership programmes in which I have been engaged highlight the importance of being proactive in sourcing learning opportunities, including mentoring and ongoing relationships with experienced leaders. The learning mentioned by the women took the form of postgraduate study, learning with and from colleagues, mentoring, as well as learning on the job. All the women acknowledged their colleagues as supportive and felt a responsibility to assist them in their own development.

Second is a *set of gender-based barriers* identified by the female participants that caused them to doubt their abilities and readiness for leadership. These barriers prevented them from either pursuing leadership or doing so in a way that caused them to doubt themselves and their abilities. Kise and Watterston (2019) identify some of these barriers including:

- different expectations for women and men that can limit their choices and decisions;
- as well as a host of barriers that women impose upon themselves such as not thinking they are ready, not applying for leadership roles because they do not have all the skills, and fearing intense criticism from others if they are not 'perfect'.

The imposter syndrome which has been associated with women aspirants and leaders was mentioned above by Nichole. She shared ways to unpack this phenomenon more objectively. I encourage you to take comfort knowing that regardless of career stage or position, most people can identify moments in their career where they may have been derailed by the imposter syndrome. As one participant in my programme shared, 'we can empower ourselves and others to step out of the imposter syndrome and our own flawsomeness'. Instead of minimising, determine and celebrate what you bring to the table.

Finally, the female participants expressed the valuable insights they gained from their involvement in the women-only programme. They expressed a profound sense of gratitude for *the opportunity to learn alongside and from like-minded women*, realising that many of the challenges they encountered on their leadership journeys were not unique to them but shared by other participants. The feedback received from AISSA indicated that this dynamic and empowering programme successfully engaged the female participants in a transformative process of personal growth, self-reflection, and collaboration, igniting their leadership aspirations.

One aspect that stood out was their commitment to paying it forward, as they embraced responsibility and dedication to actively, strategically, and intentionally supporting others in navigating the complex landscape of middle leadership. Furthermore, they pledged to reconnect and strengthen their networks, fostering confidence in themselves and their abilities, while respecting and supporting women leaders who would become strong allies in the pursuit of enhancing leadership capabilities, regardless of gender. This newfound realisation became a pivotal source of empowerment for individuals like Lucy, Nichole, Danielle, and other women in the programme.

AND NOW BACK TO YOU ...

I'm a firm believer that leadership development is everyone's responsibility, to yourself *and* others. Connecting and learning with and from others, deselecting your default (not good enough, ready enough) and paying it forward are frequently woven through the stories and anecdotes of the many women with whom I have engaged in leadership development programmes. We know that while being significant facilitators of the professional learning of others, middle leaders lack opportunities for their own development (Lipscombe et al., 2021). In the end, it is about YOU creating your own leadership identity, uniquely YOU. Leadership is about impact and influence; do you know yours?

1. Identify other leaders you admire. How have they supported you on your leadership journey and how will/do you pay it forward?
2. Write down what you would like others to say about your impact and influence?
3. What is one thing you will do because of these reflections?

REFERENCES

Kise, J. A. (2023a). Brain bandwidth: A foundation for improving educator efficacy and wellbeing. *Australian Educational Leader*, *45*(1), 8–15.

Kise, J. A. (2023b). Polarity thinking: Tools for moving forward together. *Australian Educational Leader*, *45*(2), 8–14.

Kise, J. A., & Watterston, B. (2019). *Step in, step up: Empowering women for the school leadership journey*. Solution Tree Press.

Lipscombe, K., Tindall-Ford, S., & Lamanna, J. (2021). School middle leadership: A systematic review. *Educational Management Administration & Leadership*, 1–19. https://doi.org/10.1177/1741143220983328

3

MIDDLE LEADERS CAN INFLUENCE WHAT REALLY MATTERS IN THEIR SCHOOLS

Jodie Schafer[a] and Patrick Duignan[b]

[a]Wavell State High School, Wavell Heights, Qld, Australia
[b]Australian Catholic University, Adelaide, NSW, Australia

ABSTRACT

This chapter explores the potential impact of middle leaders on their learning environments and on learning outcomes, focusing primarily on authenticity in leadership in schools. In outstanding schools, middle leaders are very active and visible in their curriculum areas, as well as more broadly around the school. They work together to build leadership capacity through the promotion of shared leadership practices based on a collective ethic of responsibility. They actively influence others to break down silos between departments and teams within a school. It is through the quality of their engagements that they project, maintain, and sustain their presence and influence with and on others. The work of authentic middle leaders is transformational insofar as they promote and support transformational teaching and learning for their students.

Keywords: Authentic leadership; head of department; trust; influence; relational leadership; silos

> **GUIDING QUESTIONS**
>
> The following are questions that you should ask yourself before you commence reading this chapter. The questions ask you to consider what you already know and feel about the topic.
>
> 1. Reflect on the leading practices you use to influence. What do you say, do, and how do you relate to others?
> 2. What actions do you take that contribute to the breaking down of silos between teams, faculties, and departments in your context?

Jodie occupies an influential middle leadership position in her school. She has reflected deeply on what seems to work and what doesn't and has developed key leadership strategies to assist her in her influential work. Her focus is on creating learning environments that encourage her students to authentically engage in learning, cultivate positive relationships with their teachers and fellow students, and seek to achieve worthwhile learning outcomes.

Patrick has researched the impact of leaders and leadership on learning environments and learning outcomes for several decades, focusing primarily on authenticity in leadership in authentic schools. He argues that leadership has long been regarded as relational, but there is more to it than simply cultivating harmonious relationships; leaders can best influence others by being fully present to and for them in relationships that have mutually beneficial outcomes.

In this chapter, Jodie and Patrick will explore what middle leaders can do to enable and enhance the depth and breadth of leadership in their schools. Jodie believes that in outstanding schools, middle leaders are highly active and visible in their curriculum areas, as well as more broadly around the school. They argue that authentic educational leaders, at all levels, challenge others to participate in visionary activities, identifying worthwhile curriculum, teaching, and learning in preferred ways of doing and acting together. Authentic leaders encourage leaders, teachers, and students to commit themselves to educational and professional practices that are, by their nature, educative; for example, encouraging and supporting conversations on goal setting, creative and innovative teaching and learning, and shared leadership.

WHAT IS AN AUTHENTIC LEADER?

Authentic educational leaders at all levels in a school work together to build leadership capacity through the promotion and support of shared leadership practices based on a collective ethic of responsibility. They engage teachers in key decisions related to the promotion of authentic teaching and learning (Duignan & Cannon, 2011). Authentic leaders encourage all who are engaged in the educational enterprise to commit themselves to quality professional practices that are, by their nature, ethically, morally, and educationally uplifting. They support teachers in bringing about innovation, especially through collective action for creative and novel teaching approaches, and they help provide resources to enhance collaborative planning for teaching and learning. Authentic educative leaders should be judged on their ability to create ethically driven, rich, engaging learning environments that break down faculty silos which can exist in some schools. Effective middle leaders adopt collaboration and consultation techniques between colleagues within and across faculties and help to create learning environments where teachers and students thrive. Such techniques are, according to Feser (2016), *influence approaches*, grouped as either 'hard or soft' tactics. Feser defines hard tactics as 'simple and straightforward tactics that leaders carry out simply by building on their own perspectives', whereas soft tactics are 'more complex and require the ability to influence based on the followers' perspectives and inner motivators' (2016, pp. 2–3). Some examples of Feser's hard and soft tactics that Jodie employs are described in Table 3.1.

Table 3.1. Hard and Soft Influence Tactics Employed by Jodie.

	Influence Approach	Examples of Effective Use of Tactic	Language Used
Hard tactics	*Requesting* – when the leader uses simple demands to get others to act	Requests to complete senior subject mark books for compliance of departmental/school policies; routine requirements	I need you to do … by … We must do …
Soft tactics	*Socialising* – leaders start to take an interest in the team members they are trying to lead; visiting staffrooms; being visible	Needed for implementation of complex tasks, for example, engaging teachers in a new pedagogical approach	How are things going with your …?
	Consultation – when the leader asks others to suggest improvements or help plan a proposed activity or change that wants or requires their support	Creates widespread commitment via connection and identification of commonalities between members of department	What are your interests outside of work?
		Gains effective clarity and direction as a team as members work through problem-solving together	What would you suggest improving …?
		Encourages initiative through trust, valuing others expertise and creating understanding between members and the middle learner	How do you see the situation?

Source: Authors' own creation.

Walumbwa et al. (2008, p. 94) defined an authentic leader as one who models:

> *[...] a pattern of leader behaviour that draws upon and promotes both positive psychological capacities and a positive ethical climate, to foster greater self-awareness, an internalised moral perspective, balanced processing of information, and relational transparency on the part of leaders working with followers ...*

They argued that positive authentic leaders inspire greater performances among all key stakeholders in their system and/or organisation. Jodie points out that when she was appointed Head of Humanities, she had been a long-term member of the faculty '... teaching alongside current team members'. Thus, the concept of being an authentic leader was 'very important to me and very necessary if I was going to be effective in my new role'. To ensure a positive ethical climate, it was important that the humanities faculty vision was a collective goal that all colleagues wanted to embrace. An implicit understanding of a faculty vision and values was evident; however, the language used to express it was inconsistent, and consequently, the core message was missing. By following Daniel Kim's (1999) 'Levels of Perspective', it was necessary for us, as a faculty, to explicitly define our vision, purpose, and values. It could have been easy, for Jodie, as the middle leader, to create a valid vision and value statement and request members to vote for its acceptance but this approach would risk 'tick a box' compliance. It would have also risked the perspective that this was an imposition from above to conform. Ensuring the creation of faculty vision and values was a collaborative effort and to inspire 'buy in', Jodie posed a series of questions to gather feedback from members. Three sample questions and their purpose are listed below:

1. Why does our faculty exist at X school? *(Clarification on our purpose)*
2. What is our 'secret sauce' that makes us a great faculty? *(Valuing the expertise among us and fundamental basis of our faculty)*
3. What do we value in our faculty for us and our learners? *(Identify key principles/mental models that underpin learning experiences)*

Developing trust, in such an activity, is vital to authentic leading, and Jodie sought techniques for collaboration that would encourage safe submission of feedback. Jodie decided she would employ technology to create a transparent collaborative feedback environment. Using the web platform Padlet at a faculty meeting enabled all voices – quiet, vocal, and new – to be captured. Padlet was also transparent and allowed anonymous feedback if desired. In-built features such as members 'liking' suggestions highlighted degrees of consensus among the team. For Jodie, the visibility that Padlet provides increased the collective consensus and therefore commitment to vision.

According to Jodie, collaboratively developing an explicit vision, purpose, and value for the faculty enhanced 'relational transparency' and set our faculty in the right direction as a more congealed group that trusted in each other. When we met, we would regularly question: 'Were the learning experiences in our classrooms meeting our vision and values? Was the assessment aligning with our purpose? Are the changes in direction for the future matching with our vision and values?'

Moreover, ensuring the faculty vision and values remain relevant, Jodie sets aside deliberate time at faculty meetings for meaningful reflection by members on the alignment between current teaching and leading in the classroom and the vision. Yearly formal reviews are also undertaken using collaborate technology platforms ensuring opportunities for participation from all. This is an example of employing 'soft tactics' rather than 'hard tactics' which, Feser (2016) argues, has better outcomes.

A challenge for middle leaders is often the addition of new members to the team throughout the year. Leave, timetable changes, and illness often mean the team at the beginning of the year is different from the end of the year with several versions throughout. Continually encouraging a collegial approach is useful when new faculty members join so that they feel they are part of a team that already has high levels of trust due to the relational transparency that exists. To manage this, Jodie again employs Feser's (2016) soft tactics such as one-on-one consultation with new members and strategic buddying with other members to build alignment between new members and the faculty vision and values.

Overall, the importance of co-construction of a faculty vision, purpose, and values cannot be underestimated in generating alignment and galvanising team members to a shared goal. The more people having a say in the creation of the vision and values, the greater the cohesive and *positive ethical climate*.

BEING AN AUTHENTIC LEADER THROUGH VALUES CLARIFICATION

Authentic educational leaders bring their deepest principles, beliefs, values, and convictions to their work. The ethic of authenticity is foundational to educational leadership as it points middle leaders towards a more self-responsible form of relationships and leadership. The authentic educational leader acts with the good of others (e.g. students, teachers, parents) as a primary reference. It is this engagement of the 'self' with the 'other' that provides the authentic educational leader with a deep sense of responsibility for what is happening to 'the other' in the school setting. This 'ethic of responsibility' is focused, primarily, on the core people (teachers and students) and the core business (teaching and learning) (Duignan, 2004).

We believe that middle leaders will be more effective when they lead with empathy, compassion, and a sense of vulnerability. Understanding that all team members are more than just teachers and have other responsibilities and lives outside of teaching is vital. Valuing people with genuine interest is essential. With wider societal discussion about prioritising work-life balance, Jodie has become more sensitive in her approach to communicating with teachers and has taken deliberate steps not to email on weekends, early mornings/late evening, respecting that communication must not become invasive in people's lives. Containing communication to more appropriate times, and careful consideration of what needs to be in emails or discussed in meetings, is a must for authentic middle leading. As well, Jodie carefully plans faculty meeting purpose and structure to ensure that unnecessary meetings are not held during peak marking or reporting times, and it is important not to have a meeting for a meeting's sake; meetings must be relevant, purposeful, and timely.

A middle leader's primary role, says Jodie, is to empower teachers to teach in a way that energises them. Effective and authentic relationships need to be *human* relationships. A middle leader can't understand how people are feeling by staying in their office. Creating genuine relationships means frequently engaging with everyone casually and individually on their terms and turf. Techniques Jodie employs to develop genuine relationships include the following:

- casually visiting staffrooms regularly and having lunch with colleagues and not always talking about work provides relationship insights;
- accepting and welcoming invitations into classrooms to help team members on their terms;
- discussing ideas either 'on the go' or deliberately with colleagues is a great way to ensure a collegial approach and sense of community; and
- having an open-door approach encourages relational transparency and avoids people feeling isolated and undervalued.

A middle leader can utilise Feser's (2016) *soft tactic* of socialising, to build rapport, identify commonalities, and match behaviours or conversational pacing. Further to this, typical statements by a leader using socialising tactics are:

- I am very impressed by what you have achieved.
- That really shows lots of commitment and dedication. It would be great if you could ....
- I see the problem the same way.

To enhance the ulitisation of soft tactics Jodie deliberately set aside time so faculty members could voluntarily identify their strengths using a survey tool. Jodie then created time and space after school for team members (with the support of a dedicated leadership consultant Steve Francis, 2020) to unpack the survey findings together. Jodie believes that working together to understand individual strengths and therefore the team's collective strengths has helped inform efficient and enjoyable ways of relating with each other to achieve faculty goals. Through such interactions, a middle leader deepens their understanding of fellow team members and therefore how best to interact with each member to achieve more effective outcomes.

DISCUSSING AND SHARING IDEAS

A welcoming open-door approach is essential to encourage the sharing of ideas and adds to *relational transparency*. Jodie shares her vulnerabilities as a teacher and middle leader, which makes her more than happy to relay areas where she is struggling; retelling of what did or did not go well for her is important for building trust. This often leads to interactions of shared practice where all parties can learn from each other – a discussion of equals. In addition, discussions both informally and during meetings, ensure Jodie uses terms such as 'we' and 'us' rather than 'I'.

Inviting and deliberately making time to discuss ways to achieve these goals is important to Jodie. Rather than assuming suggestions from team members won't work, Jodie asks encouraging questions about how *members* think it will work, what they are hoping to achieve, and how she can help. Jodie believes in the adage of 'far more is gained by having a go and failing than not having a go'. Such a mindset displayed by faculty members will overflow into classrooms where students will also be exposed to a growth mindset.

INFLUENCING AND AUTHENTIC LEADERSHIP

Inspirational and authentic leaders understand others' perspectives because they focus on what lies deep in other people's mindsets, that is, their values and emotions. Influential leaders use this tactic to appeal to people's values and ideals or seek to ignite team members' commitment to a request or proposal. Keeping this in mind when socialising with faculty members, Jodie strategically appeals to specific team members' values and strengths to motivate them to embark on new and exciting ways of advancing key aspects of students' learning experiences. This makes team members feel valued and is also influential on faculty members. A leader using inspirational appeals might say:

- Because you care so much about X, would you consider taking on and developing this project.
- 'You're the best one to handle this ... because you care about this issue the most ...' (Feser, 2016, p. 6, chapter 3).

A middle leader's positive outlook about teaching and learning is contagious and encourages action from like-minded members. It is important to have a strong, passionate belief in teaching the subjects within your faculty and regularly display this. Ask yourself, 'how could I be an authentic leader if I do not love what I do and believe in it'? 'As a Humanities leader, I must see value in teaching humanities subjects', says Jodie. This adds to 'positive psychological capacities'. Effective and optimistic communication between faculty members leads to work being achieved without it feeling like work. Cameron (2008) claims that engaging with positive energisers '... leaves others feeling lively and motivated, builds energy in people and is an inspiring experience' (p. 42). Duignan's *Legacy Paper* (2014) identified the key elements of positive school cultures as '... positive emotion, engagement, meaning, positive relationships, and accomplishment' (p. 16). In the words of educational leadership expert, Dr Neil Carrington (2021), you need to become a Chief Affirmation Officer (CAO) telling members they are 'doing great at X and their expertise in Y is fantastic' builds positive relations and energy in the faculty. Obviously, affirmations must be genuine and sensitive and delivered with sincerity.

Authentic leadership also involves doing the work that team members will grapple with. Rolling up the sleeves (so to speak) together to tackle the 'new directives' from educational organisations builds trust and authenticity in experiences. Whether it be a new version of the Australian curriculum or total transformation of senior secondary exit requirements, being in among the change that fellow members will experience gives valuable opportunity to build trust and relationships. It also provides avenues for influence.

Recognition that not all team members will see the vision from the same perspective as you and or fellow members is worth considering. Having worthy rivals is essential to ensuring that all options are considered and that faculty members do not become an echo chamber of your thoughts only (Carrington, 2021). To be a more effective relational leader, you must be open to challenges and prioritise time to allow for self and peer reflection – not everyone will have the same perspective as you, and you need to be open to challenges or risk the failings of confirmation bias. Only associating with members who agree with you or not investing time to allow critical reflection from members creates a one-dimensional faculty having one-dimensional outcome. An effective way to ensure multiple perspectives, says Carrington (2021), is that the middle leader should talk last or at least give their opinion last to really hear what the team wants or thinks. Providing opportunities for dissenting opinions to be discussed safely and respectfully develops trust.

CREATING AUTHENTIC TEAMS BY BEING AN AUTHENTIC LEADER

Jodie encourages individuals and work teams in her areas of influence to take greater responsibility for the continuous improvement of leading the faculty. She noticed the problem that faculty meetings were becoming too centred around her, because she ran faculty meetings by physically standing at the front of the classroom. It was effective but not empowering. She reflected on some of the following questions and invited feedback from colleagues:

- How could meetings be more member orientated and member run?
- How could they be less hierarchical?
- Did all meetings have a clear purpose and were members clear on, and supportive of, this purpose?
- What was the role of the head of department (HOD)/middle leader at these meetings?

After self-reflection, Jodie sought solutions from members to make faculty meetings more purposeful. She wanted to continue to create 'a positive ethical climate' and wanted colleagues to want to be at meetings because they saw value in them. Again, Jodie used the soft tactics of consultation and socialising and incorporated technology to assist her to gather feedback on:

- Why do we have meetings?
- What would you like to see at meetings – including physical layout/people?
- How would you like to feel at meetings and how can this best be achieved? (Energised, valued?)
- How can we better achieve what we want out of meetings?
- What does not need to be at a meeting?

As a result of the feedback, the faculty meeting format was changed. On a rotational basis, team members were:

- given the role of chair or moderator; to read the faculty vision and values, outline the agenda, and provide key 'take aways' at the end;
- invited to share pedagogical practice and contribute ideas; and
- encouraged to celebrate student and teacher leadership in curriculum.

Eliciting member contribution at meetings flowed best from using Feser's (2016) soft tactic of 'socialising'. Casually visiting with members was a great way to see and hear about extraordinary pedagogy that was happening every day. The excitement of seeing this through *socialising* compelled Jodie to want other members to see what was happening in their own team. Recognising the wealth of knowledge and talent that sits within and among team members allows for effective and ongoing professional development. Opportunities were also strategically provided to allow for cross-faculty members to present, signifying that their contribution was valued. Shared practice contributes to building trust, adding to authentic relationships.

The new meeting format provided opportunities to share teaching experiences from teachers who were both new and experienced. When doing this for the first time, Jodie would 'tee it up' with members who, she thought, would be willing to take on the roles; she had a trial run first to ensure a smooth and engaging approach. Once it was modelled in a fun and simplistic way, it was easy getting members to take on these roles, and this approach has become very successful. After some time, it became apparent that these meetings could be run even without the HOD needing to speak or take the leading role. On one occasion when Jodie was unable to attend a meeting due to illness, the meeting still went ahead without her, adding to the sense that this was a faculty meeting of equals. These member-driven solutions, facilitated by the middle leader, enhanced member ownership of faculty meetings and avoided meetings being dissemination of information from above.

Further adding to a positive ethical climate, part of being an authentic leader is to celebrate the achievements of all members professionally. Regular acknowledgement of member successes, whether they be derived from awards or the 'silent success' of teaching in the classroom, constitutes valid recognition that fosters a sense of everyone's worth. Acknowledgement can be given publicly and explicitly through communication at meetings, emails, and special gatherings or through quiet conversations of appreciation and acknowledgement. Even a handwritten note of thanks can also go a long way for those who prefer quiet recognition.

CULTIVATING AUTHENTIC RELATIONSHIPS

Numerous writers on leadership over the years have pointed out that leadership is essentially relational (e.g. Duignan, 2006; Fullan, 2005; Halpern & Lubar, 2004). Patrick believes that many educational leaders tend to neglect this leadership imperative because they operate in challenging and complex environments where the urgent becomes important. They are, frequently, distracted by the hectic pace of school life and eschew opportunities for reflective analysis on the quality of their relationships and on the deep learning required to bring about transformation in self and others. Investing in significant relational time getting to know team members is much more worthwhile in the long term in achieving a dynamic and empowered faculty. Knowing team members strengths and values and trusting in them through shared leadership practices allows the middle leader to be confident that everyone is working to a shared goal. As famous mindset coach Ben Crowe (2020) instilled often in elite tennis player, Ash Barty, it is more about the 'human being rather than the human doing'.

According to Jodie, 'allocating deliberate time for and creating opportunities to reflect on member relationships and build trust has been instrumental in achieving shared understandings of the why and what in the department and therefore the acceptance of changes to improved teaching and learning'.

Many leaders find it difficult to engage more fully with others in their workplaces because they may lack the emotional intelligence to be open, trusting, and authentically reciprocal in their relationships. Those driven by corporate, bureaucratic, hierarchical, and other managerial imperatives may have no room in their hearts for valuing and respecting the integrity of others and engaging with them to enhance the quality of their work environments. An obsession with performance outcomes may rob them of the generosity of spirit that is a hallmark of authentic and transforming leadership. Of course, schools need to be managed efficiently and effectively, and organisational members must be held accountable for the quality of their performance, but it does not mean that all this cannot be achieved within ethical, professional, respectful, and compassionate environments.

Patrick advocates that developing relationships based on integrity, trust, and respect for the dignity and worth of others is a prerequisite if middle leaders hope to maximise their influence on those within their fields of influence. It is through the quality of our engagements that we project, maintain, and sustain our presence and thereby our influence with and on others. The work of authentic educational leaders is transformational as far as they promote and support transformational teaching and learning for their students. To do this, they must bring their deepest principles, beliefs, values, and convictions to their work.

Leadership has long been regarded as relational, but there is more to it than simply being physically present in the present moment with others. Teachers are authentically present when they have deep engagement with their students. Such engagement awakens them to the sacred and reflective space that exists between them. Reflection is the key to establishing deep engagement and authentic action.

REFLECTION TASK

An effective, authentic leader is self-aware and is deliberate in choosing what they say and do. Over time, Jodie has developed the pillars of her authentic leadership. Writing this chapter has helped her clarify and express these pillars. Here they are:

Jodie's Authentic Leadership Wisdom for middle leaders:

- Leaders should talk last or at least give their opinion last to really understand what the team wants/thinks.
- Employ technology to create genuine collaborative environments and seek feedback.
- Set time aside in meetings for regularly questioning or affirming the vision and values of the faculty.
- It is important not to have a meeting for a meeting's sake; meetings must be relevant, purposeful, and timely.
- Understand team member strengths and use them to the team's advantage.
- Creating genuine relationships means frequently engaging with everyone casually and individually on their terms and turf.
- Use soft tactics to build relationships and create a trusting culture.
- Share vulnerabilities as a teacher and middle leader.

Steps:

1. Take 15 minutes to write down your list of authentic leadership practices. What do you do and say that helps you create positive relationships with your team?
2. Store your ideas somewhere.
3. Come back in three months' time to reflect on, refine, and change your ideas.

MIDDLE LEADERS CAN HELP BREAK DOWN SILOS IN SECONDARY SCHOOLS

In a recent book, *Leading Educational Systems and Schools in Times of Disruption and Exponential Change*, Patrick Duignan (2020) described the challenges and opportunities for leaders in a VUCA world – a world of volatility, uncertainty, complexity, and ambiguity. He posed several questions, especially on secondary schools' capacity to deliver the type of education required for students to excel in times of frequent disruptions and rapid changes:

- What forms of education and schooling will best prepare secondary students for 21st-century VUCA conditions?
- Are there systems and schools nationally and internationally that are 're-forming' in response to these conditions?
- Are there developments from outside education that provide examples of how other organisations or businesses have successfully changed to meet 21st-century demands?

One major lesson Patrick learned from a review of relevant literature is that even very successful organisations can and do fail. Outside of education, he discovered that successful health, business, and other organisations have transformed themselves by embracing new architectures, structures, purposes, processes, and information technologies. Gans (2016) asked the question: 'Why do very successful companies, continuing to do what made them successful, eventually end up failing?' Despite its great success over decades, *Encyclopaedia Britannica* collapsed due to strong disruptive forces coming from newer companies such as Microsoft, Wikipedia, and Apple. Kodak and Blockbuster Video also collapsed due to the emergence of digital cameras and Netflix.

Tett (2015) analysed the role of silos in organisations during the global financial crisis of the early 2000s. She claimed that prior to 2008, many bankers did not appreciate the risks they were taking because they lived in a banking world where different teams of financial traders '... did not know what each other was doing, even inside the same ... institution'. Tett used the example of Facebook as a company that was aware, from the beginning, of the negative effects of silos so, as a result, the Facebook platform '... enabled communication to occur in a horizontal way, instead of via a rigid hierarchy'. When somebody made a post, everyone could access that piece of information; in contrast to the usual communication patterns where information tended to get passed up or down hierarchies, creating potential bottlenecks and logjams' (p. 226).

Patrick provides useful example for school middle leaders of teamwork, positive information flow, and the demolition of silos. He gives the example of *The Cleveland Clinic* in the United States where Toby Cosgrove became CEO in 2004 and announced that he was going to implement '... two big revolutions' (reported in Tett, 2015, p. 252). He argued that it was time for the hospital's 43,000 staff to

> *[...] rip up their existing taxonomy for defining a 'doctor' or a 'nurse' all the staff would now be considered 'caregivers', responsible for not just treating the physical ailments but the spirit and emotions as well; he set about changing how the hospital was organised. (pp. 252–253)*

Instead of the traditional organisation of *departments* and *doctors*', he redefined it around '... the patients and their illnesses' by creating new *multidisciplinary* institutes, thereby forcing '... surgeons, physicians, and others to work together in treating patients' (p. 253). On 1 January 2008, Cleveland Clinic announced its *Big-Bang Revolution* – 27 new *Institutes* were created (p. 258) clustered around such broad labels as 'Digestive Diseases Institute', 'Head and Neck Institute', 'Heart and Vascular Institute', and 'Cancer Institute'. In 2013, a survey of patient satisfaction stated, '... *Cleveland Clinic* was the top-ranked hospital in America in terms of patient satisfaction' (p. 264). President Obama lauded the Cleveland Clinic as a place '... where patients' care is the number-one concern, not bureaucracy' (Tett, 2015, p. 264).

Both Jodie and Patrick believe that these outcomes of the Cleveland Clinic have implications for middle leaders in secondary schools and secondary education. Based on the lessons from the *Cleveland Clinic*, as well as their own experiences in secondary schools in Canada and Australia, they both conclude that educational leaders can learn a great deal about silos and how to reform them from successful examples in other systems and organisations. Jodie is very aware that as a middle leader of a department, it would be easy to turn inwards and focus only on her own department's needs and interests. 'We, as middle leaders, should not operate in boxes', says Jodie. '... our schools and universities put students into boxes at a young age, and academic departments are fragmented' (Tett, 2015, p. 314). Both Jodie and Patrick believe that one key message we can derive from organisations that have effectively transformed their silos is that our schools do not function effectively if they are always rigidly organised and streamlined. Tett (2015) suggested that '... living in specialised silos might make life seem more efficient in the short term, but a world that is always divided into a fragmented and specialist pattern is a place of missed opportunities ...' (p. 315). Both Jodie and Patrick believe that educators and educational leaders can learn many practical leadership lessons from companies that have re-*formed* their silos. Middle leaders can not only motivate team members to embrace a shared faculty vision; it is important as well that middle leaders collaborate with other faculties to ensure alignment. One faculty working in isolation from others could lead to misalignment of the overall school vision. If middle leaders are to do the best for their students, then it is better for faculties to work to complement each other rather than compete.

They pose the question: Could all secondary school staff be considered 'educational caregivers', responsible for treating or educating the whole person, the spiritual and emotional dimensions as well as the educational ones? Instead of internal silos in secondary schools, organised around subjects and departments, why couldn't they be reorganised around students' learning needs and developmental stages? Could secondary schools be reorganised as 'multidisciplinary institutes' and thus require leadership teams, including teachers and other educational assistants, to work together in educating their students? Could we regard schools as places where students' care is the number-one concern and then change the architecture for learning, accordingly? Educators and educational leaders wishing to break down silos and transform educational architectures can learn many practical leadership lessons from the business organisations we discussed.

As a middle leader, Jodie believes that middle leaders will have a crucial role to play in bringing about this transformation of structures and services. As Wilson (2018) stated so eloquently: 'there is no single model to follow when it comes to redesigning space and the schedule' [but] '... it is important to start with the curricular and pedagogical priorities first, before rethinking and redesigning the use of time and space' (p. 54). Such changes will require smart, agile leaders and leadership.

A MODEST PROPOSAL FOR THE MIDDLE LEADER

Julie Wilson, a great American researcher on quality teaching and learning, is very hopeful of a bright future for education. Based on her research across many hundreds of American schools, she has personally observed:

> *teams of teachers, school leaders, students, parents, and whole communities collaboratively and creatively transforming their educational learning environments and experiences for students;*
>
> *many school environments being reimagined and redesigned to unleash the potential of both teachers and students and to invite learners to think for themselves and take ownership of their own learning; and*
>
> *[...] a rising army of hundreds of thousands of people doing something about it – with humility, with heart, and with faith. (p. 107)*

Both Jodie and Patrick want to be part of this army of thousands, and they hope that the discussions and conclusions in this chapter will encourage you, too, to join and become a positive force for the transformation of our educational systems and schools as well as for the life opportunities of our current and future students.

REFERENCES

Cameron, K. (2008). *Positive leadership: Strategies for extraordinary performance.* Berrett-Koehler Publishing.

Carrington, N. (2021, July 22). *The most important thing leaders should do: Ace leadership masterclass with Dr Neil Carrington.* Carrington Consulting Group.

Crowe, B. (2020). Mojospresso Ep 08 human – Being vs doings. *YouTube*. https://www.youtube.com/watch?v=hJFAYMZ0zDw

Duignan, P. (2004). William Walker oration: The insight and foresight of Bill Walker – Motorcycle maintenance 30 years on (1974–2004). *Australian Council for Educational Leaders Monograph Series*, *25*, 4–16.

Duignan, P. (2006). *Educational leadership: Key challenges and ethical tensions*. Cambridge University Press.

Duignan, P. (2014). Authenticity in educational leadership: History, ideal, reality. Legacy Paper. *Journal of Educational Administration*, *52*(2), 2014.

Duignan, P. (2020). *Leading educational systems and schools in times of disruption and exponential change: A call for courage, commitment and collaboration*. Emerald Publishing Ltd.

Duignan, P., & Cannon, H. (2011). *The power of many: Building sustainable collective leadership in schools*. ACER Press.

Feser, C., & Vries, M. K. (2016). *When execution isn't enough: Decoding inspirational leadership* (foreword by M. K. Vries). Wiley.

Fullan, M. (2005). *Leadership and sustainability: Systems thinkers in action*. Corwin Press.

Francis, S. (2020). The importance of strengths based leadership. https://stevefrancis.au/theimportance-of-strengths-basedleadership/

Gans, J. (2016). *The disruption dilemma*. The MIT Press.

Halpern, B. L., & Lubar, K. (2004). *Leadership presence: Dramatic techniques to reach out motivate and inspire*. Penguin Books.

Kim, D. H. (1999). *Introduction to systems thinking*. Pegasus Communications, Inc.

Tett, G. (2015). *The silo effect: Why every organisation needs to disrupt itself to survive*. Abacus, Little, Brown Book Group.

Walumbwa, F. O., Avolio, B. J., Gardner, W. L., Wernsing, T. S., & Peterson, S. J. (2008). Authentic leadership: Development and validation of a theory-based measure. *Journal of Management*, *34*(1), 89–126.

Wilson, J. M. (2018). *The human side of changing education: How to lead change with clarity, conviction, and courage*. Corwin.

4

DEVELOPING MIDDLE LEADERS IN CATHOLIC SCHOOLS

Michael Harrison and Louisa Rennie

Melbourne Archdiocese Catholic Schools (MACS), Melbourne, VIC, Australia

ABSTRACT

This chapter explores the development of middle leaders in the specific context of Catholic schools. It considers the interplay between contemporary thinking on educational leadership and the insights of Catholic theology and ministry. Two key themes foundational to this interplay are examined: the connection between leading and following, and the central importance of relationships for leadership. For each of these themes, the reader is provided with related questions for middle leaders in a Catholic school context, an activity for engaging with leaders, and an exercise inviting middle school leaders to reflect on their own experience and the context within which they lead.

Keywords: Middle leadership; leader; follower; Catholic schools; theology; ministry; discipleship; human dignity; relationships; mission

GUIDING QUESTIONS

The following are questions that you should ask yourself before you commence reading this chapter. The questions ask you to consider what you already know and feel about the topic.

1. Leading is a dance of leading and following. What does it feel like for you to be a leader and a follower?
2. What is your leadership mission?

THE CHALLENGE FOR CATHOLIC SCHOOLS

In recent years, there has been increasing discussion related to the Catholic identity of Catholic schools, both in Australia and abroad. This chapter specifically explores the experience in Melbourne, Australia, where the governing body, Melbourne Archdiocese Catholic Schools (MACS), has direct responsibility for over 300 primary and secondary schools and liaises with 30 plus secondary colleges governed independently by religious orders or boards. It is a significant education system supporting at least 152,000 students and 17,000 staff.

The context of this discussion is complex. In past years, Catholic school systems relied primarily on an inherent Catholicity where staff and students in any given school community lived out their Catholic faith within their own families and in local parishes. Regular attendance at mass and adherence to Catholic traditions and rituals was more commonplace in those times.

The present circumstance, as exemplified in the Melbourne Catholic education experience, is different and evolving. There has been an increasing secularisation of Australian society in the past 30 years as religious experience has become less central to the lives of some citizens. The practice of Catholicism has also been affected by the historical child sexual abuse crisis. And so today, as long-standing Catholic teaching staff are retiring, a new generation of teachers coming into Catholic schools do not have a formative lived experience of Catholic faith. Catholic education systems can no longer rely on an inherent Catholic understanding in their staff or their families to implicitly form the Catholic identity of the school, parish, and community. The Australian Catholic Bishops recently stated that:

> *As Catholics in Australia become increasingly diverse in the practice of their faith, it would appear that an extraordinary event or events would need to occur before we witness a reversal – or even a plateau – of the declining attendance trends. There would need to be a surge in younger people attending Mass, or the unanticipated arrival of large numbers of Catholics from overseas, to offset the advancing age profile of attenders. (Australian Catholic Bishops, 2016, p. 15)*

For Catholic systems and schools, the challenge exists to make the previously assumed and implicit Catholic identity of schools far more explicit, and this has ramifications for leadership development. How leaders can be truly Catholic leaders, and how this leadership in a Catholic context is different from secular and other religious school systems, is at the heart of programs now being explored within the context of Catholic education in Melbourne: 'Catholic leadership is synonymous with leading a community of faith. It encompasses the capacity to articulate a clearly defined vision for the future, inspiring others to follow' (CEM, 2019, p. 3).

Middle leaders such as assistant principals, department heads, and curriculum coordinators play a crucial role in shaping the culture and climate of all schools. Australian Institute for Teaching and School Leadership (AITSL, 2023) notes that 'middle leaders and middle leadership practices have become increasingly recognised as significant factors in the success of Australian schools' (AITSL, 2023). They are often responsible for leading specific initiatives such as the implementation of new curriculum, well-being policies and programs, or the development of professional learning opportunities for teachers. As such, middle leaders are crucial for continuous school improvement and the development of a safe environment where learning and learners can flourish.

In Catholic schools, middle leaders also play a key role in ensuring that the Catholic mission and values of the school are woven into the fabric of the school community and are reflected in the experiences of students and staff. This is not separate to their leadership role but intertwined into all that they do. It is at the core of the way they behave, their interactions with others, the choices they make, and the way they lead. For Catholic identity to be sustained, and in fact thrive, middle leaders need to be developed as role models and advocates for other teachers and staff members, as their actions and behaviours influence the way in which the Catholic identity of the school is lived out on a day-to-day basis.

To sustain and deepen understanding of Catholic identity and to ensure that it permeates a vision for a relevant and thriving future for Catholic education, MACS has identified that a particular focus on middle leadership is essential in supporting schools to effectively fulfil their mission and provide a high-quality Catholic education for all students.

ACTIVITY 1: WHAT ARE THE ISSUES?

Key Questions

1. From your perspective, what challenges does Catholic education face that are specific to Catholic schools?
2. How do these challenges affect being a leader in a Catholic school?
3. What are the responsibilities of Catholic school leaders regarding the Catholic identity of their schools?
4. What responsibilities relate generally or specifically to the role of middle leader in a Catholic school?

Journal Reflection

In what ways are you affirmed by this discussion related to your responsibilities as a Catholic school middle leader, and in what ways are you challenged?

Suggested Activity

Explore the key questions in a professional learning group using the 'fishbowl' protocol.

https://www.gse.harvard.edu/sites/default/files/Protocols_Handout.pdf

CATHOLIC MIDDLE LEADERS' PROGRAM

MACS is committed to the design of professional learning that is fit for purpose, personalised to the Catholic context, and tailored to suit the learning needs of middle leaders (Gurr & Drysdale, 2012; Irvine & Brundrett, 2016). MACS is therefore exploring the development of a program for middle leaders in Catholic schools that is inherently Catholic in content design and delivery. The program:

- is content focused and context relevant;
- incorporates active learning and engagement;
- supports transfer of knowledge and understanding to inform practice;
- is job-embedded;
- uses models and modelling of effective practice;
- provides coaching, peer, and expert support;
- offers opportunities for feedback and reflection;
- is of sustained duration; and
- is research informed and outcomes focused (Fluckiger et al., 2015; Sawyer & Ramirez-Stuckey, 2019).

Ways Forward

The present circumstances and challenges facing Catholic education call for a wholistic and nuanced program. The Catholic identity of schools begins with a commitment to mission and values and works its way through to specific school policies and programs. The interplay between the teachings and practices of the wider Catholic Church community, the expectations and regulations of the appropriate secular authority, and the broader developments in educational theory and practice are central to the living out of this shared mission in Catholic schools. The National Catholic Education Commission (NCEC, 2017) states that '… formation for mission [in Catholic education] is a process that is systematic, collaborative, graduated and ongoing. The process holds itself within relationships built on accompaniment centred on the self, other, creation and God' (p. 14).

The core mission for Catholic schools is to cultivate discipleship transformed by the sacred teachings of Jesus. This requires leaders to focus on personal growth '… in spiritual awareness, theological understanding, vocational motivation and capabilities for mission and service in the Church and the world' (NCEC, 2017, p. 9).

TWO KEY THEMES FOR CATHOLIC LEADERSHIP

A major intention of the program is to integrate Catholic theology and educational leadership understanding and practice. This is exemplified in the two themes explored below.

To Lead Is to Follow … To Follow Is to Lead

Most organisations are familiar with the idea of 'mission', and this is often accompanied by a mission statement which explores 'vision' and 'values'. It is recognised that we work best when we can identify not just where we are going, but why we are going there, and what part we play in this venture. A mission statement should both inspire and hold to account those who are part of a school community – students, staff, and families. For leaders in the school, it is both an aspiration and benchmark for their work, and this is particularly important for middle leaders. Dinham et al. (2018) state that '… leadership [today] is increasingly being seen as a group function, occurring when two or more people interact in the pursuit of ... a desired outcome' (p. 14).

The idea of 'followership' is relevant to middle leadership for several reasons. To lead others, middle leaders need to bring people with them. This requires the leader to be convincing, to have an evidence informed strategy, to be consultative, to listen, to influence the behaviour of others, to lead from and beyond the middle, and to accompany people on that journey. At times, this might mean handing over to another or simply recognising the co-leadership that might be occurring. In following an inspirational leader, one is encouraged to take on those leadership traits and put them into action in their own context. In high-performing cultures, the leader and the follower are in-sync, and the lead role can interchange. This can be observed in networks where leadership is distributed and shared.

Middle leaders must be able to develop and maintain positive relationships with all members of the school community, including teachers, staff, students, and parents. This again requires the ability to be a follower as well as a leader. Having a keen sense of self and an awareness of one's capabilities also enables the middle leader to know when to follow others. Middle leaders will, therefore, benefit from self-assessment as a core component of any middle leadership program. This is evident in times of ideation and brainstorming, where school leaders contribute to shaping future directions, together. Working collaboratively and being responsive to the needs and perspectives of others in the school community is a key leadership behaviour for middle leaders.

Grice (2022) states that high-performing leaders recognise how it felt to be a follower and employ strategies to be mindful of that perspective and the value it can bring to decision-making and moving forward and '... when change has been brought about, leaders and their communities assume improvement, or even transformation' (p. 30). It is not the leader alone who moves forward because forward movement needs to occur together if change or continuous improvement is to occur.

The Catholic tradition considers followership from a Catholic perspective. It speaks of the mission of the Church and the mission of Catholic schools as part of this. And it speaks of discipleship rather than followership. Just as the Gospels describe those who followed Jesus as his disciples, the Church has continued to use the idea for all those who have committed their lives to the mission of the Church. The concept of discipleship therefore becomes fundamental to Catholic education and has correlations with the idea of 'followership', particularly in terms of living by example and building positive relationships. Lowney (2007) observed:

> *We Christians … call ourselves 'followers' of Jesus, and our religious language uses words with connotations of followership, like 'disciple' and 'vocation'. The Latin root of 'disciple', for example, connotes a pupil or follower. But our religious language also uses words with the opposite connotation, like 'apostle' and 'mission'. The roots of these words connote 'sending'. And when I send you somewhere, you are not following; you're striking out and forging the way ahead. That's the dynamic of Christian life: we lead and follow. (p. 34)*

The Catholic tradition provides guiding wisdom for leaders in Catholic schools about how to be a Christian disciple. Pope Francis has spoken often in his papacy about the idea of 'missionary disciples': 'Every Christian is a missionary to the extent that he or she has encountered the love of God in Christ Jesus: we no longer say that we are "disciples" and "missionaries", but rather that we are always "missionary disciples"' (Pope Francis, *Evangelii Gaudium*, para. 120). In this statement, Pope Francis is recognising that all those working in Catholic organisations, schools included, are part of the broader mission of the Church and, as such, have the responsibility to understand the teachings and values of the Church's mission, to apply those teachings and values as 'disciples' and to take this into their ministry. Catholic school leaders are called to be disciples who take the mission of the Church to the staff they are working with and to the students and the wider school community.

Anthony Gittins (2016) identifies four characteristics of Christian discipleship which he traces back to the ministry of Jesus. He argues that missionary disciples need to exhibit these characteristics in recognition of our shared responsibility to continue the mission of Jesus in our work and daily interactions:

Encounter: Jesus actively reaches out to encounter others in their lives. True encounter involves meeting people in their daily lives. Catholic leaders are challenged to listen deeply to the stories of others and to find and value their unique contribution to the community and its mission.

Table-fellowship: A key component of Jesus' ministry was the frequency with which he is described as sitting at a table with others. In his time, as in ours, sitting at table was a sign of respect and affection. Catholic leaders are called to not just walk with others but to minister to them with hospitality – whatever that might mean in a school and team environment.

Foot-washing: Jesus and his disciples walked dusty roads, and so a key component of hospitality was to wash a visitor's feet as they entered a home, a role normally reserved for servants. Peter's discomfort at the Last Supper when Jesus motioned to do this for him (John 13:3–9) shows how this was regarded at the time. Catholic leaders are called to this form of humble ministry, often referred to as servant leadership in the tradition.

Boundary-crossing: Christians are called to reach out to the peripheries of our communities. In both his words and his actions, Pope Francis has been consistent in applying a long history of Catholic Social Teaching to advocate for those at the margins, and this has significantly influenced Catholic educational thought. The foundational 'Horizons of Hope' Vision and Mission Statement has a foundational vision to 'honour equitable access and opportunity for all, with a particular commitment to those most in need' (CEM, 2019, p. 6).

ACTIVITY 2: LEADING AND FOLLOWING

Key Questions

1. How does the idea of leading and following relate to leadership in a Catholic school?
2. The role of middle leader is often described as a balance between leading and following. How do you experience this in your daily work?

3. In what ways are you affirmed by this discussion related to your responsibilities as a Catholic school middle leader, and in what ways are you challenged?

Journal Reflection

For each of the four characteristics of Christian discipleship identified by Gittins (2016), write an affirmation of where you have successfully engaged with the characteristic in your leadership and a challenge for yourself where you could extend your leadership.

Suggested Activity

Explore the key questions raised by Gittins (2016) in a professional learning group using the 'jigsaw' protocol, with each group focusing on one specific characteristic.

a) Encounter
b) Table-fellowship
c) Foot-washing
d) Boundary-crossing

https://www.gse.harvard.edu/sites/default/files/Protocols_Handout.pdf

Relationships are Everything

The dignity of each human person is central to Catholic moral and social teaching. The teaching references the first creation story in Genesis where God creates humans 'in his image, in the image of God he created them; male and female he created them' (Genesis 1:27). This understanding is extended in the Christian tradition with the theology of the Incarnation, the belief that Jesus Christ is both fully human and fully divine. In Christian understanding, if

God has been sent into the world in human form, in all its fullness and fragility, then every human person has a worth beyond measure and must be treated with the dignity appropriate to this.

The earliest recognised papal encyclical on Catholic Social Teaching (Pope Leo XIII, *Rerum Novarum*, 1891) focuses specifically on the dignity of the human person in terms of their work, and how each person finds dignity or not within their work. Catholic thought has built on the ideal of the dignity of the human person in all aspects of life ever since. It is not surprising then that building relationships and recognising the dignity of the human person are key themes for Catholic education and should inform the practice of middle leadership in the Catholic context because

> *Leaders believe that everyone can experience success and be supported to see their lives as being shaped by the God who is at work in all of creation. Leaders privilege each person's sacred right to flourish and become all that they may dream to be. (CEM, 2019, p. 9)*

Educational leadership exists within the very relationships that are forged in schools. And it is through those relationships that middle leaders can exercise influence and lead change. Rincon-Gallardo (2022) suggests this is three-directional:

> *[...] they liberate downwards by creating the conditions to liberate learning for and alongside those they lead; they interact laterally with other peer leaders, to learn from and contribute to their colleagues. As well as to create collective capacity and power to move a shared agenda forward; and they leverage upward by being proactive in their interaction with the system leadership above them – both leveraging existing system strategies and policies in the service of their local agendas and exerting influence on policy design and implementation. (p. 190)*

Considering middle leaders in this way sheds light on the power and potential that exists in their leadership and strengthens the resolve to invest in them, so they are well positioned to lead with maximum effect. In a similar vein, Buchanan et al. (2022) observes that for middle leadership:

> *[...] relationships, interpersonal skill, collegiality, cooperation, and teamwork must be recognised as quintessence in the role regardless of its intended outcome – line-manager, professional colleague, or faith-mentor. From this perspective, building collegiality, cooperation and teamwork should not be only part of middle leadership but, rather, be its core practice. When based upon trans-relational values and principles, all aspects of Catholic school middle leadership are founded on mutually beneficial, and thereby strongly influential, interpersonal relationships. (p. 309)*

It is important for Catholic leaders to consider the way in which Jesus most deeply affected people. It is understandable that we are drawn to Gospel passages as a one-off encounter, whether that be the healing of individuals or the forgiveness of others or extraordinary encounters such as the Samaritan woman at the well described in John's Gospel (Jn 4:1–26). However, as powerful as these encounters obviously were for those involved, Jesus' deepest teaching happens within the community of apostles and disciples who followed him. And while Jesus is often portrayed as calling the apostles and disciples aside from the crowds to teach them, it is not difficult to see that it is living with him in a relationship and seeing his witness to his mission that has the most profound affect. José Pagola (2015), in his expansive historical reconstruction of Jesus' life, explains the effect on his apostles and disciples of living in relationship with Jesus as leader:

> *something new is awakening in the hearts of the disciples. That contagious peace, that purity of heart without a trace of envy or ambition, his ability to forgive, his acts of mercy in the face of weakness, humiliation or sin, his passionate struggle for justice on behalf of the weakest and most abused, his unbreakable trust in the Father. All this is awakening in them a new faith .... (p. 278)*

He further observes that:

> *[...] there are two characteristics that Jesus nourishes among his followers: the equality of all, and loving service to the last. This is the legacy he wants to leave: a movement of sisters and brothers in service to the smallest and most helpless. (Pagola, 2015, p. 279)*

It is for these reasons that the Catholic tradition has always strived to trace itself back to those apostles, who did not just hear the message preached but saw it enacted in each moment of Jesus' life. They knew like no other that this mission was dependent on witness and relationship, and that is the leadership style they took into the development of the early Christian communities (see Acts 2:42–47).

ACTIVITY 3: BUILDING RELATIONSHIPS

Key Questions

1. How important to leadership in a Catholic school is building relationships?
2. Buchanan et al. (2022) argue that 'building collegiality, cooperation and teamwork' should be the key concern of the Catholic school middle leader? Do you agree?
3. What are the limitations for leadership when relationships are neglected?
4. In what ways are you affirmed by this discussion related to your responsibilities as a Catholic school middle leader, and in what ways are you challenged?

Journal Reflection

How do you build relationships as a leader, and how do you manage specific relationships when you need to challenge others? Explore an example from your experience and identify things that you might now change in your approach as a leader. What might you do differently?

Suggested Activity

Explore the key questions in a professional learning group using the 'concentric circles' protocol.

https://www.gse.harvard.edu/sites/default/files/Protocols_Handout.pdf

CONCLUSION

This chapter has outlined the way in which MACS, a significant Catholic education system, is seeking to design a fit-for-purpose program for middle leaders in Catholic schools which builds on contemporary educational leadership research and Catholic social teachings. The program will seek to both respond to the inherent needs and extend the knowledge, understanding, and practice of middle leaders across the Archdiocese.

In doing so, it has identified areas of Catholic thought and practice which would enable middle leaders to effectively develop their leadership in ways which are authentic to the Catholic identity of their school communities. This includes a commitment to the Catholic educational mission, the realisation that the ideal of Christian discipleship imbues all aspects of Catholic leadership, and the need to build genuine relationships that respect the dignity of all.

REFERENCES

Australian Catholic Bishops. (2016). *Australian Catholic mass attendance report 2016.* National Centre for Pastoral Research Conference.

Australian Institute for Teaching and School Leadership. (2023). *Middle leadership in Australian Schools.* AITSL. www.aitsl.edu.au/research/spotlights/middle-leadership-in-australian-schools

Buchanan, M. T., Branson, C. M., & Marra, M. (2022). Bringing purpose and peace-of-mind to the role of a Catholic school middle leader. *British Journal of Religious Education, 44*(3), 304–314.

Catholic Education Melbourne. (2019). *Leadership in a Catholic school.* Horizons of Hope Foundation Statement.

Dinham, S., Elliott, K., Rennie, L., & Stokes, H. (2018). *I'm the principal: Principal learning, action, influence and identity.* ACER Press.

Fluckiger, B., Lovett, S., Dempster, S., & Brown, S. (2015). Middle leaders: Career pathways and professional learning needs. *Leading and Managing, 21*(2), 60–74.

Gittins, A. J. (2016). *The way of discipleship: Women, men, and today's call to mission*. Liturgical Press.

Grice, C. (2022). Leading forward by salvaging for the future. In D. M. Netolicky (Ed.), *Future alternatives for educational leadership*. Routledge.

Gurr, D., & Drysdale, L. (2012). Tensions and dilemmas in leading Australian schools. *School Leadership and Management*, *32*(5), 403–420.

Irvine, P., & Brundrett, M. (2016). Middle leadership and its challenges: A case study in the secondary independent sector. *Management in Education*, *30*(2), 86–92.

Lowney, C. (2007). *Everyone leads*. Rowman & Littlefield.

National Catholic Education Commission (NCEC). (2017). *A framework for formation for Mission in Catholic Education*. https://ncec.catholic.edu.au/wp-content/uploads/2022/12/AFramework4FormationMission.pdf

Pagola, J. A. (2015, Rev.). *Jesus: An historical approximation*. Convivium Press.

Pope Francis, Evangelii Gaudium, The Holy See. https://www.vatican.va/content/dam/francesco/pdf/apost_exhortations/documents/papa-francesco_esortazione-ap_20131124_evangelii-gaudium_en.pdf

Pope Leo XIII, Rerum Novarum, The Holy See. https://www.vatican.va/content/leo-xiii/en/encyclicals/documents/hf_l-xiii_enc_15051891_rerum-novarum.html

Rincon-Gallardo, S. (2022). Leading to liberate learning; educational change meets social movements. In D. M. Netolicky (Ed.), *Future alternatives for educational leadership*. Routledge.

Sawyer, I., & Ramirez-Stuckey, M. (2019). *Professional learning redefined: An evidence-based guide*. Corwin.

COLLABORATING AND COMMUNICATING

5

RELATIONAL TRUST AS COMMUNITY BUILDING PRACTICE

Jessica Pound[a] and Christine Edwards-Groves[b]

[a]Catholic Education Diocese Wagga, Wagga, NSW, Australia
[b]Griffith University, Nathan, QLD, Australia

ABSTRACT

Middle leaders are educators whose practices of building relational trust are critical for generating the kind of strong and sustainable professional learning communities necessary for leading productive site-based education development in their school. This chapter specifically focuses how building an ethic of relational trust, experienced in five interrelated dimensions, aligns with establishing core foundational conditions for building community. Building trust and communities of professional learners are not mutually exclusive – in fact, each reciprocally facilitates, progresses, supports, and sustains the development of the other. The foundations for community building, described as cornerstones, form over time and progressively involve, and achieve, contextuality, commitment, communication, collaboration, criticality, and collegiality. Reflection questions are provided throughout; these are designed to directly focus the attention of middle leaders towards understanding and developing their own trust practices, that with time, create conditions for generating strong viable communities of professional practice.

Keywords: Relational trust; cornerstones; ethic of trust; community of practice; practice architectures; site-based education development

GUIDING QUESTIONS

The following are questions that you should ask yourself before you commence reading this chapter. The questions ask you to consider what you already know and feel about the topic.

1. What is the relationship between building relational trust and establishing strong communities of professional practice?
2. In what ways are the specific cornerstones for building community implicated in the practices of middle leading?

> *When I began my role as a school-based literacy leader, I instinctively knew that the foundation to building a community of professional learners was (is) developing relational trust. This was critical for both the success of the initiative within my diocese, but also my own development as a middle leader. Getting started was challenging, but my first wondering was how does trust and community building work in reality? Second, how does a genuine sense of community develop and be sustained?*

This chapter explores one teacher's journey to middle leading (author Jessica) through the focus on the interconnected realms of trust and professional learning communities. It draws together ways the five dimensions of relational trust, identified by Edwards-Groves et al. (2016), connect with seven cornerstones necessary for fostering the development of a strong community of professional learners (Edwards-Groves & Rönnerman, 2021). Building trust and communities of professional learners are not mutually exclusive – in fact, each reciprocally facilitates, progresses, supports, and sustains the development of the other.

FACILITATING AN ETHIC OF TRUST FOR BUILDING AND SUSTAINING STRONG COMMUNITIES OF PROFESSIONAL LEARNING

Middle leaders are educators intricately entangled in the leading, professional learning and teaching practices of their school. Their work is critical in contributing to the landscape of professional learning in schools simply because they predominantly exercise their leading in and around the teaching and learning that happens in classrooms, where their responsibility is often to guide and lead professional learning among their colleagues (Grootenboer, 2018; Grootenboer et al., 2014, 2020). Edwards-Groves et al. (2020) have described the leading work of middle leaders as creating possibilities for generating shared transformational practices among groups of colleagues in schools.

The fundamental premise of this chapter is that professional learning and building a community of professional learners is intricately connected to, and almost reliant on, an *ethic of trust* (Edwards-Groves et al., 2016; Möllering, 2006, 2013). An ethic of trust is driven by a strong sense of the site (context) and a shared commitment to pedagogical excellence that reciprocally supports enhancement in student learning. Specifically, this chapter examines what an ethic of trust entails in practice, particularly in relation to the critical role middle leaders have in building strong pedagogical teams that form sustainable and productive communities of professional practice. It puts the focus on what this means for middle leaders, since a large body of educational trust centres on how principals build trust with their staff (Kutsyuruba & Walker, 2014; Northfield, 2014). Through vignettes describing and reflecting on middle leading (written by middle leader and author, Jessica), we consider ways trust and community building are reciprocal, mutually enhancing, interconnected features of *site-based education development* (Kemmis et al., 2014) and evolve as a *dynamic, multi-dimensional social process* (Grootenboer et al., 2020).

Arriving at a sustainable and productive community of practice requires strategic and deliberate practices designed to create communicative spaces (both formal and informal) on the part of the middle leader (Rönnerman et al., 2018). In fact, open communicative spaces among professionals have been shown to be necessary for building communities of practice (Malloy, 1998) but reciprocally generative of leading practices (Edwards-Groves & Rönnerman, 2013; Rönnerman & Edwards-Groves, 2012). Communicative spaces are the engine room for facilitating the formation of professional learning relationships, which reciprocally enables the emergence of a community of practice (or not). A communicative space is *a public sphere* where teachers and middle leaders, as a collective of learning professionals, come together as interlocutors (people in dialogue with one another) to engage with their profession through foundations of commitment, communication, collaboration, criticality, and collegiality (Edwards-Groves & Rönnerman, 2021). As Edwards-Groves and Rönnerman (2021) found, these foundations are cornerstones which directly and deliberately respond to the context where one is situated at the time and are necessary for transforming the practices of individuals in ways which facilitate the formation of strong viable community (of professional practice). It is in facilitating a culture of relational trust that middle leaders are uniquely positioned to leverage productive school-based education development (Edwards-Groves et al., 2016). The relational imperative of professional learning requires an ethic of trust emboldened by distinctive kinds of supportive leadership practices; thus, leading the practice development of others requires creating conditions that foster relational trust.

UNDERSTANDING THE CONDITIONS FOR CREATING A CULTURE OF RELATIONAL TRUST

Edwards-Groves and Rönnerman (2021) showed in their longitudinal research reporting the journey from teaching to middle leading that it was a generative socially constitutive process that begins with a deep understanding of the context, and through iterative processes of commitment, communication, collaboration, criticality, and collegiality, a community of practice evolves

(Edwards-Groves & Rönnerman, 2021; Lave & Wenger, 1991). That is, a professional learning community is not a *fait accompli* simply by virtue of a program, initiative, or policy, nor because one calls it such. What is required is knowing about the site-based conditions, local circumstances, and the particularity and distinctiveness about the practices which constitute a particular context (Grootenboer et al., 2020); this is a central imperative for building a community of professionally committed practitioners.

Specifically, in their research, Edwards-Groves and Rönnerman (2021) found that a sense of community is the ultimate accomplishment of working professionally together and can only be developed if those persons present are genuinely committed to collaborate and communicate openly with one another over time, are responsive to their contexts, and where being openly critical rest on one's experiences of collegiality, collaboration, and communication with others (Edwards-Groves & Rönnerman, 2022). They described these foundations as cornerstones which form necessary what Edwards-Groves et al. (2010) described as *relational architectures*, which site-responsive conditions for building professional learning communities. These conditions are presented and explained briefly next in Fig. 5.1.

As Edwards-Groves and Rönnerman argued, each cornerstone is in an indissoluble relationship with the other and forms influential conditions (or practice architectures, Kemmis et al., 2014) for the development of the other. Over time, the extent to which a community of professional learning is accomplished relies on demonstrating and acknowledging how each is 'integral' to forming an indispensable intrinsically connected part of the development of the other. This point is taken up in Jessica's reflection here:

> *I soon realised that a community of practice didn't just magically appear because we were all working towards the initiative or just because we were interested in improving the literacy outcomes of the school ... I couldn't take this for granted ... I had to figure out how a community develops and what my role as a middle leader meant in it.*

What holds each of these cornerstones in place is **trust**. As Grootenboer and Edwards-Groves (2021, p. 1) asserted, trust is

Contextuality – a cornerstone for site-based education development;

Commitment – a cornerstone for individual and collective change;

Communication – a cornerstone for participation and shared meaning making;

Collaboration – a cornerstone for collective action;

Criticality – a cornerstone for critical inquiry and activism;

Collegiality – a cornerstone for sustainability; and

Community – a cornerstone for democratic ways of working.

Fig. 5.1. Cornerstones for Building Community.
Source: Adapted from Edwards-Groves and Rönnerman (2021, p. 52).

the relational glue that holds together a professional learning community. This insight about trust is critical for middle leaders, since their work leading the learning of colleagues is inherently relational. As Edwards-Groves et al. (2016) found, trust is a dynamic multidimension relational practice delineated in five distinct, yet interrelated, realms (summarised and exemplified next). These dimensions, and their realms of focus, have been adapted and expanded from the combined original work by Edwards-Groves et al. (2016) and subsequent research conducted by Edwards-Groves and Grootenboer (2021). The reflection questions following each dimension are designed to support middle leaders consider what each means for their own leading work (these were drawn out as reflection questions by Jessica, inspired from the research paper by Edwards-Groves et al., 2016).

1. *Interpersonal dimension* relates to a middle leader's character and disposition – where they demonstrate approachability, empathy, care, acceptance of difference and teacher colleague expertise, mutual respect, and trustworthiness; relate to others responsively and genuinely; and engender confidence and empowerment among teachers.

To develop as a middle leader, I must continually reflect on my own relatability, by asking myself:

- How do I relate to others in my team?
- Am I trustworthy?

- Am I recognised by my colleagues as a leader who is trustworthy?
- Am I seen by others as trusting of the members of my team?
- Do I demonstrate genuine empathy, and relate to, respect, and engender confidence in my teaching team?
- At a deeply personal level, do my colleagues feel that I understand them, and am I genuinely interested in them as valued colleagues?
- Do I foster diversity of roles and functions within a shared purpose, goal, or mission, where each member is respected and appreciated for their part in the team?

2. *Interactional dimension* concerns communication and communicative spaces – where middle leaders create open and safe spaces for interthinking, cooperation, dialogic integrity, collaboration, and democratic dialogues among teacher participants.

To develop as a middle leader, I must continually reflect on my own interactional practices, by asking myself:

- How do I interact with others?
- In what ways can and do we collaborate?
- Do I open and sustain safe spaces for collaboration and democratic dialogues?
- Do team members feel confident, comfortable, and valued in expressing their professional ideas and contributing to the team performance?
- Do I feel comfortable facilitating open dialogue where all ideas and views are welcomed, heard, and considered?
- Do I feel confident enough to lead and guide coaching and mentoring conversations in such a way that is a supportive and safe space for my colleagues?

3. *Intersubjective dimension* relates to a community of shared focus and practice – where middle leaders demonstrate 'withitness', consensus, and collegiality through shared language, a

productive dialogic culture, sensemaking, problem-solving, activities, and community because they, too, are invested in the change agenda for their own teaching development.

To develop as a middle leader, I must continually reflect on my own dialogic and collegial practices, by asking myself:

- How do I work with others?
- Am I a genuine part of the team?
- Am I genuinely journeying with the teachers in my team?
- Am I working at the elbow as a fellow professional?
- Do I demonstrate collegiality through participating in the shared learning activities?
- Do I really appreciate and understand their individual and collective problems, issues, and struggles?

4. *Intellectual dimension* involves recognition of expertise and academic competence, where middle leaders convey self-confidence, professional knowledge, expertise, and wisdom regarding the focus of the development work.

To develop as a middle leader, I must continually reflect on my own knowledge and professional learning practices, by asking myself:

- How do I share my expertise and equally recognise the expertise of others?
- How well do I know my stuff?
- Do my team members perceive me as knowledgeable, wise, and having expertise?
- Can my team trust me to convey self-confidence, professional knowledge, and wisdom regarding the developmental work we are focused on?
- Do I engage in ongoing professional learning and development for myself?
- Is there confidence and trust that I 'know what I am talking about'?

5. *Pragmatic dimension* encompasses the situated relevance and practical work of middle leaders – where middle leaders lead activities and professional learning agendas in ways that are practical, relevant, realistic, and achievable.

To develop as a middle leader, I must continually reflect on the practical realities of what I am asking teachers to do, by asking myself:

- How do I recognise and account for the needs (of this community, school, teachers, and students) and the circumstances under which this initiative is being rolled out?
- Is the work doable and worth doing?
- Can I be trusted to drive the team, but not overwork or overwhelm them?
- Can they trust that the work we are doing together is valuable and worthwhile to their professional improvement?
- Is the work relevant to the teachers and ultimately their students?
- Have I been realistic in the time allocated to accomplish the learning goals required of the initiative?
- Have I provided sufficient time for teachers to practice or trial the new strategies or approaches so that what is expected of them is manageable and rewarding?

Each of these dimensions of trust is entangled in the social exchanges, mutually understood responsibilities and designations, and interactions and relationships formed among key stakeholders in schools (Edwards-Groves & Grootenboer, 2021, p. 264). Yet critically, each is critical for building strong, and so sustainable, communities of learning professionals. We represent the interconnection between building trust and its relationship to building community next in Fig. 5.2.

The cornerstones, outlined previously, form an interconnected basis for considering ways middle leaders support teachers in their schools to '*act in*, *act on*, and *act for* their profession'

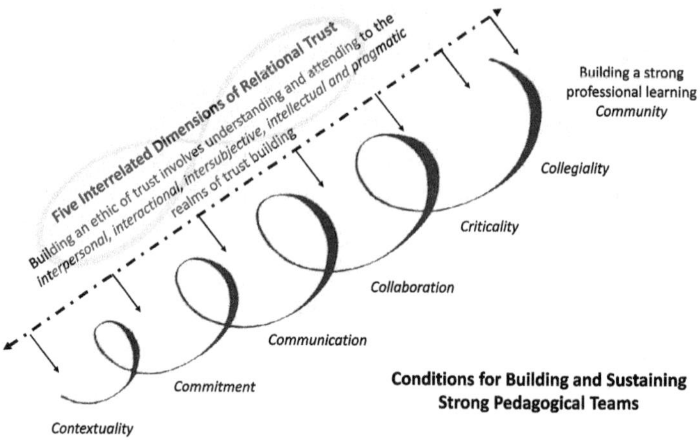

Fig. 5.2. Cornerstone-Trust Spiral: The Conditions for Building and Sustaining Strong Pedagogical Teams.

Source: Authors' own creation.

(Edwards-Groves & Rönnerman, 2021, p. 52). Here, relational trust, in its five interdependent dimensions, is imbricated in teacher's individual and collective development whereby the practice of middle leading empowers them to actively engage in professional learning.

MIDDLE LEADERS LEAD WITH TRUST

Recently, Edwards-Groves and Grootenboer (2021, p. 279) asserted that middle leaders lead with trust. In fact, leadership is intensely relational work (Helstad & Møller, 2013). In respective studies about middle leading practices in primary (Edwards-Groves et al., 2015) and secondary schools (Edwards-Groves & Grootenboer, 2021, p. 279) showed ways that:

> *[…] trust for professional change is entangled in relational practices experienced in interpersonal, interactional, intersubjective, intellectual, and pragmatic realms. The inseparability of five dimensions of relational trust forms the distinctive multidimensional nature of*

> *the relational building blocks that encompass dynamic, interconnected and interdependent social-political resources for leading change – each simultaneously forming and transforming the intersubjective spaces in which teachers participating in school-based change engage ... practitioner engagement involved a relational doubleness, where relational trust not only formed conditions for middle leaders to consciously protect and preserve communicative spaces for developing trust, but that each dimension is necessary for building and sustaining a coherent community of practice. This, at the same time, generated necessary conditions required for realising the transformational goals of professional learning in the schools.*

It is through trust that middle leaders work towards a community of professional learning practice (Niedlich et al., 2021). However, it is important to consider that it is through this trust that middle leaders can do the necessary work for building a community, but at the same time, they must recognise and establish each of the cornerstones in their own local context.

SEVEN CORNERSTONES THAT BRING COHERENCE TO THE FOUNDATIONS OF MIDDLE LEADING

The cornerstones – contextuality, commitment, communication, collaboration, criticality, collegiality, and community – form composite, interrelated practices that rely on relational trust for their development. Although the cornerstones are tightly interconnected, they are only made a real part of the professional learning experience in a school if trust is developed alongside the middle leader's day-to-day activities. One cannot build a genuine 'community' without trust that is supported over time by deliberate attention to the other cornerstones as formative and transformative conditions for the successful implementation of professional development initiatives in place. Community building is dependent on relational trust, where there is a direct relationship connection between building a strong professional community or effective and collaborative teaching teams. It is relational trust that binds the cornerstones together, which are not only interconnected but formed simultaneously where arriving at a sustainable and embedded community of practice. Thus, building strong professional communities of practice is a process (Jagd, 2010) that requires equal attention to both the multiple dimensions of relational trust and the cornerstones.

AN EXAMPLE FROM THE FIELD

Through working in one of the classrooms, Jessica noticed that there were some disconnections between student understanding and teacher practice. To arrive at a place of creating sustainable change within this classroom, a solid foundation of trust had to be developed between her (Jessica) and the classroom teacher. She noticed that the development of trust is not bound by a timeframe, rather it is through her imperative work of reflection on her own work as a middle leader that focused on what was happening, why weren't things working and how can she open effective yet trusting dialogue with her colleague[s]. This led her to reconsider her actions, starting with throwing out one-size-fits-all approaches she was using, and realising where the breakdown of trust lies. She began by asking – Are we on the same page? Have we got consensus or a shared commitment about what we are doing together? Arriving at this new starting point, she thought about how she can develop trust through facilitating more empathetic and person-centred actions appropriate for each teacher's own development through the cornerstones of commitment, communication, and collaboration. She realised this took time and take days, weeks, or months, depending on the individual colleague. But in the end, this is time worth taking.

The cornerstones are not a linear process for middle leaders to tick off as checkboxes, rather they should be seen as embedded processes of middle leading practices that are fundamental to the success of building a strong, sustainable, trusting, and, thus, effective community of professional practice. At each point along the continuum to building a genuinely successful community (through the phases aligned with the cornerstones), the dimensions of relational trust must be reflected upon and actioned by the middle leader. Without the deliberate generation of trust throughout the process, weak links are created in the cornerstone spiral (see Fig. 5.2), and thus, the capacity to work towards a community of professional practice becomes threatened, fragile, and flawed. An awareness of the cornerstones, as well as demonstrating continued attention on the work that nourishes relational trust in each of the dimensions, provides middle leaders the optimal conditions to create, build, and sustain an effective and productive community of practice.

THEORY INTO PRACTICE: SELF-REFLECTION QUESTIONS FOR BUILDING STRONG TRUSTING TEAMS

To conclude, the fundamental to the success of middle leaders in their work is the innate ability to reflect on continuously and consciously one's own professional strategies and learning with consideration of trust within the cornerstones (also refer to reflection questions within the vignettes above).

Recognising **contextuality**

As a middle leader do I have strong consideration for my school site and are my strategies specific to the site, the school, the staff, and the students?

In my role as a middle leader, do I provide thoughtful and pertinent substance to the professional learning I create, develop, and deliver for my staff?

How can I authentically understand and learn the needs and requirements of my context?

Establishing shared **commitment**

As a middle leader, how am I both morally and professionally committed to my role and my team?

What are the conditions necessary to create teacher 'buy in' and trust in the educative work we are doing together?

Opening spaces for **communication**

In my communicative actions (e.g. coaching/mentoring conversations, leading staff meetings/professional learning, reflection groups) as a middle leader, how do I create a respectful, yet democratic space for open, safe, and productive dialogical conferences to occur?

Through my interactions as a middle leader, do I facilitate both a physical and social space whereby there is opportunity for shared meaning and language to be supported?

Negotiating **collaborative** ways of working

Are my colleagues provided with opportunities for co-planning, co-creating, and co-constructing in search for a shared purpose and the collective action within their own and others' practice?

Embracing **criticality**

Through my work as a middle leader, do I and my colleagues engage in critical reflection and critical inquiry dialogue in relation to our educative work?

Consolidating **collegiality**

Through bouncing through the cornerstones of commitment, communication, collaboration, and criticality, middle leaders can arrive at a point where it is made possible for both themselves as middle leaders and their staff to accept and generate critique in their dialogue about initiatives or classroom practice, therefore becoming a collegial team. Consolidating this sense of being collegial means the commencement of a solid foundation of a community of practice.

ARRIVING AT A STRONG COMMUNITY OF PRACTICE

How do I recognise my colleagues' work and celebrate our community?

When each of these cornerstones is fundamentally in place, it is now possible to arrive at a place of community. However, it is important to nourish and protect this important work at each stage through critically reflecting on each of the cornerstones to determine effectiveness of the work. It is imperative that this fundamental work of the middle leader, through the cornerstones, is not taken for granted. It must be nurtured and nourished to not just arrive at a community of practice but for it to be sustained and maintained and embedded into the culture of the school context.

REFERENCES

Edwards-Groves, C., & Grootenboer, P. (2021). Conceptualising the five dimensions of relational trust: Middle leadership in schools. *School Leadership and Management*, *41*(6), 1–24.

Edwards-Groves, C., Grootenboer, P., & Rönnerman, K. (2016). Facilitating a culture of relational trust in school-based action research: Recognising the role of middle leaders. *Educational Action Research*, *24*(3), 369–386.

Edwards-Groves, C., & Rönnerman, K. (2013). Generating leading practices through professional learning. *Professional Development in Education*, *39*(1), 122–140.

Edwards-Groves, C., & Rönnerman, K. (2021). *Generative leadership: Rescripting the promise of action research*. Springer.

Edwards-Groves, C., & Rönnerman, K. (2022). Action research conceptualised in seven democratic cornerstones: Reinstating the historical core for critical inquiry, rethought purposeful action, and systematic responsive development in education. *International Journal of Action Research*, *18*(2), 24–40.

Edwards-Groves, C., Wilkinson, J., & Mahon, K. (2020). Leading as shared transformational practice. In K. Mahon, C. Edwards-Groves, S. Francisco, M. Kaukko, S. Kemmis, & K. Petrie (Eds.), *Pedagogy, education, and praxis in critical times* (pp. 117–141). Springer.

Grootenboer, P. (2018). *The practices of school middle leadership. Leading professional learning*. Springer.

Grootenboer, P., & Edwards-Groves, C. (2021). *Trust: Relational glue*. https://www.griffith.edu.au/engage/professional-learning/content-centre/trust-leadership-glue

Grootenboer, P., Edwards-Groves, C., & Rönnerman, K. (2014). Leading practice development: Voices from the middle. *Professional Development in Education*, *41*(3), 508–526.

Grootenboer, P., Edwards-Groves, C., & Rönnerman, K. (2020). *Middle leadership in schools: A practical guide for leading learning*. Routledge.

Helstad, K., & Møller, J. (2013). Leadership as relational work: Risks and opportunities. *International Journal of Leadership in Education*, *16*(3), 245–262.

Jagd, S. (2010). Balancing trust and control in organizations: Towards a process perspective. *Society and Business Review*, *5*(3), 259–269.

Kemmis, S., Wilkinson, J., Edwards-Groves, C., Hardy, I., Grootenboer, P., & Bristol, L. (2014). *Changing practices, changing education*. Springer.

Kutsyuruba, B., & Walker; K. (2014). The lifecycle of trust in educational leadership: An ecological perspective. *International Journal of Leadership in Education*, *18*(1), 106–121.

Lave, J., & Wenger, E. (1991). *Situated learning: Legitimate peripheral participation*. Cambridge University Press.

Malloy, K. (1998). *Building a learning community: The story of New York City Community School District #2*. Learning Research and Development Centre, University of Pittsburgh.

Möllering, G. (2006). *Trust: Reason, routine, reflexivity*. Elsevier.

Möllering, G. (2013). Trust without knowledge? Comment on Hardin, 'Government without trust.' *Journal of Trust Research*, *3*(1), 53–58.

Niedlich, S., KallfaB, A., Pohle, S., & Bromann, I. (2021). A comprehensive view of trust in education. Conclusions from a systematic literature review. *Review of Education*, *9*(1), 124–158.

Northfield, S. (2014). Multi-dimensional trust: How beginning principals build trust with their staff during leader succession. *International Journal of Leadership in Education*, *17*(4), 410–441.

Rönnerman, K., & Edwards-Groves, C. (2012). Genererat ledarskap [Generative leadership]. In K. Rönnerman (Ed.), *Aktionsforskning i praktiken – förskola och skola på vetenskaplig grund [Action research in practice]* (pp. 171–190). Studentlitteratur.

Rönnerman, K., Edwards-Groves, C., & Grootenboer, P. (2018). *Att leda från mitten – Lärare driver professionell utveckling [Leading from the middle – Teachers driving professional development]*. Lärarförlaget.

6

LEADING OUT, TO LEAD IN: DEVELOPING IN THE ABSENCE OF STRONG LEADERSHIP

Steven Kolber[a] and Stephanie Salazar[b]

[a]*The University of Melbourne, Melbourne, VIC, Australia*
[b]*Sanctuaries of Learning, NSW, Australia*

ABSTRACT

Teachers are an adaptive group of professionals and in this chapter, we explore the ways that teachers can develop themselves as leaders, even in the absence of strong support or leadership. We explore the manner that these skill sets and strengths can be cultivated, providing lived examples of how the authors have developed themselves. The ways that teachers can follow in the footsteps of the authors is outlined in clearly defined steps. By drawing on previous literature, we provide seven strong claims of developing middle leadership knowledge and skill sets beyond your school. Much of this development and community development work that develops and sharpens leadership skills can be explored through online fora and social media tools. These tools allow skill development, professional learning, and exposure to a broad range of education stakeholders and groups; for future pathways in school leadership roles and leading beyond school gate.

Keywords: Leadership; social media; teacher excellence; activism; professional learning; empowerment

GUIDING QUESTIONS

The following are questions that you should ask yourself before you commence reading this chapter. The questions ask you to consider what you already know and feel about the topic.

1. If you could have anyone in the world as a mentor, who would you choose?
2. What is your pedagogical or leadership gift? What's something you care about more deeply than others?
3. What would you provide in return to such a mentor?

INTRODUCTION: WHAT IF I AIN'T GOT LEADERSHIP'S SUPPORT?

De Nobile (2018) notes six core conditions for middle leader success: principal support, professional development, culture, enthusiasm, drive, and knowledge. While this advice is valuable, it develops an expectation of perfect conditions for which leaders are expected to grow and flourish. Good leadership, a collegial school culture, and good professional learning (PL) are three attributes that many teachers desire; they are all fleeting and difficult to attain across a system where these elements may differ widely and be hard to find. Here, we explore the ideas of what happens:

1. In the absence of high-quality leadership.
2. Within a staffroom lacking in pedagogical discussions.
3. Where high-quality PL is uncommon.

Much of our careers have revolved around the following questions: to whom do you turn in the absence of high-quality leadership?

Where do you go when your staffroom is not abundant with pedagogical discussions? Where and how might you participate in high-quality PL? The answer to each of these questions will be discussed, in turn, below, assuming their very absence within your own setting. You might think, some of these three challenges are present in my school, or some of the six features that De Nobile (2018) expects are present where I work. Perhaps some of these elements once existed but have not been sustained. This is true of all careers, and all school settings, so we can avoid a half-filled glass viewpoint and still strive for greatness in our work.

Scholars (Benson, 2021; Dinham, 2016; Duignan, 2012; Southworth, 2008) note that the work of leaders is about influencing others via vision sharing, direction setting, and motivating. While the importance of context is supreme in all matters of leadership, aspirational middle leaders can practice these three skills by leveraging online spaces and social media to elicit these types of responses from teachers and education-invested individuals beyond one's own school.

Within our middle leadership roles, we echo the sentiments of Grice (2019) whose metaphor is that middle leaders are most like a spy, working between the leadership team, the teaching staff, and in the grey space of policies and practices, within the broader systemic culture (Kolber, 2022). The grey spaces of policy and practice and working between competing challenges within schools has some clear parallels with teachers working online. We feel that engaging in PL online, leading, sharing, and collaborating is superb for developing cultural capital and beginning to understand your capability to influence up, down, and sideway: but most of all to develop a greater understanding of self: your own set of skills, how you influence, how you manage change, areas for growth, and how you lead collaboration. Though many a leadership development course will call for the writing of a 'leadership manifesto' to outline the 'why' of your leadership journey, online engagements can be a means to enact and practice your leadership manifesto instead of merely committing it to paper. As we know, leadership is a verb, rather than a nominalised zombie noun.

OVERCOMING THE CHALLENGES TO GROW AND BLOOM

While this chapter is framed in the negative, both authors have been blessed to work with excellent leadership at different points and stages of our careers. Indeed, as middle leaders develop across their careers, they take on different nuances and seek out different kinds of support. For Stephy, she felt different to other beginning teachers at her school when she first started because she was eager to attend and organise PL opportunities for new teachers in the community outside of school hours. She accepts now that this deep commitment to becoming a better teacher for students is simply part of who she is as an educator. 'Leading out' by finding ways to facilitate events for teachers in the broader community enabled Stephy to effectively lead inwards and at her school.

As West (2022) notes, the infighting embedded within the teaching profession and the way social media can be a means of accelerating some of these concerns, as noted elsewhere, there is 'no referee' online (Carpenter & Harvey, 2019). We do not brush aside the concerns among scholars of increased risks for teachers having an online presence. Indeed, as noted within Barnes (2021), lost jobs and court cases are distant, though real possibilities for teachers' online activities, and not a risk to be taken upon without first heeding this warning.

As Bressman et al. (2018) note, the early career stage is filled with 'survival mode' tactics, while the mid-career stage sees teachers move beyond their own concerns towards a focus on students' learning; finally, the late career stage sees teachers deepen expertise and gain a broader view of education. It may well be interesting for readers to consider which stage they find themselves in, as each stage holds a different requirement for support and leadership. Though this is especially true if you are supporting teachers across these stages in your middle leadership roles.

One important element here is the affordances of social media, the things that it allows that cannot be achieved within schools themselves, even though they often contribute to them.

While the concern of this type of online 'thought leadership' can be viewed as 'aspirational labor' (Duffy, 2017; Yallop, 2021), with gendered overtones, tapping into neoliberal expectations of 'working at something you love', in a way that never results in actual paid work. The flaws and nature of leadership development mean that this could be one of the few ways to develop the skills and attributes of a strong educational leader. Indeed, Barnes (2021) notes that leaders within schools should be on the lookout for ways to benefit and leverage the skills of educational social media producer's skillets, rather than viewing these practices as inherently dangerous and of concern. Nicoll (2022) suggests that using social media PL within initial teacher education (ITE) can develop skills there and then the communities developed by them will sustain teacher mentoring and support beyond these years. Alongside Nicoll (2022), we echo the sentiment that: 'perhaps being an influencer isn't such a bad thing?' (p. 1).

WHAT'S POSSIBLE? (THINGS WE'VE DONE THAT ARE COOL)

While it might seem on the surface self-serving, we feel it important to outline some outcomes of the types of work we have completed, including how the process begins personally and leads to collective actions and representation, as an illustration of what is possible and how the process occurs. Fig. 6.1 succinctly outlines our view of such a process.

This is important because as our work shows clearly, working on individual, or collective projects online develops and sharpens skill sets that have real relevance and importance within the education ecosystem. This is especially true, since teacher representation

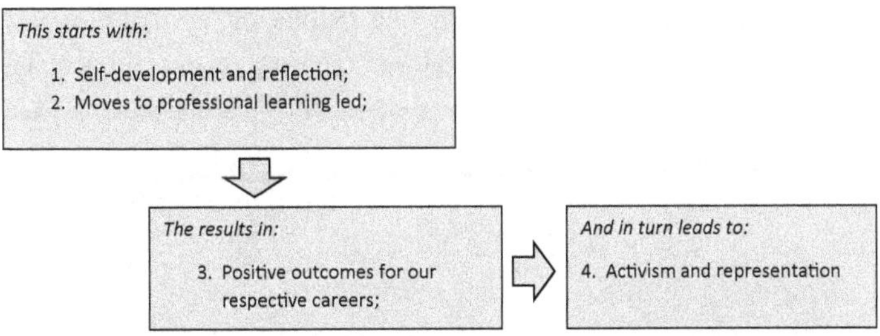

Fig. 6.1. The Process and Movement From Self; to Collective; to Activism and Representation.

Source: Authors' own creation.

in the media tends to be negative, problematic, and challenging (Mockler, 2022; Shine, 2018, 2020), thus making positive teacher-led representation and activism of crucial importance. Though we note that this may never be the goal or express purpose of any of this work, it's useful to foreshadow the possibility of activism and representation of teachers and the profession. Lastly, you can remain confident that if you progress to this step, just as with attaining leadership positions, you will be well prepared and eloquent in both because of the work that led up to either.

SELF-DEVELOPMENT AND REFLECTION

Podcasting Into Speaking

Stephy has podcasted with the Teachers' Education Review (TER) podcast and TeachNSW; Steven with the TER podcast. The importance of speaking regularly on the work of teaching and leadership cannot be underestimated, leading to speaking at online (Kolber, 2020) and face-to-face Teach Meets (Bryceson, 2012; Esterman, 2011, 2015; Salazar, 2022), conferences, and as per the goal of this chapter, presenting to whole-staff and small group sessions within your own school context.

Blogging/Writing

Steven's micro-blogging (tweeting) lead to a blog, *The first 100,000 words: writings on education,* where he continues to develop his craft of writing and seen his writing published across many of the major educational publications, including academic articles and most recently the publication of the book that he co-edited with Keith Heggart: *Empowering Teachers and Democratising Schooling: Perspectives from Australia* through Springer Nature (Heggart & Kolber, 2022).

Through tweeting Stephy has been able to reflect with inspiring educators about teaching and leadership. She started sharing photos of lessons during her practicums as a pre-service teacher as well as reflections from PL sessions she attended. She now continues to share photos of the many teachers and leaders she works with as well as PL opportunities she designed as a middle leader. Fortunately, she was invited to contribute a chapter to Steven and Keith's book, titled: *Welcome to the New Teacher Tribe: Empowering Beginning Teachers by Co-creating Sanctuaries of Learning*.

Professional Learning Led

Running Twitter chats is an accepted form of online PL leadership that sees the leader providing questions in a time-sensitive (usually an hour) manner for audience participants to respond to. The chat leader administers these questions, encourages, retweets, and asks questions to further draw out information from participants. These online practices require many skills of leadership, including seeking consultation, responding to different approaches to teaching and leadership and many more soft skills besides.

#PSTchat has been running actively on Twitter since 2013, including taking on new hosts such as experienced middle leaders, Angie Taylor, and Dr Sandy Nicoll.

The #newteachertribe hashtag naturally evolved to connect new teachers and supportive teachers and leaders online. A guide on how to replicate its success can now be read in every university library in Australia (Salazar, 2022).

Steven's #edureading group takes a particular interest in educational research, reading an academic article a month, sharing short video responses via FlipGrid, before finally culminating in an hour-long Twitter chat. This hybrid model mimics the models of Professional Learning Communities and a Community of Practice Model, which are extremely common within schools. As such, the matter of participant buy-in is highly important and has proven an effective way to draw out differences of opinion around key educational debates. This group has both produced research (Kolber et al., 2021) and remains an ongoing research site, seeking to locate what has made this methodology so effective (Campbell, 2022; Kolber & Heggart, 2021; Mercieca, 2021; Mercieca & McDonald, 2021).

Positive Outcomes for Our Careers

Stephy has moved into a Leadership Coaching role, moving from middle leadership into leadership 'proper'. She has worked at sustaining her school's coaching programme by engaging middle leaders in coaching cycles and then providing feedback during their coaching cycles with beginning teachers. Stephy also took a break from the primary classroom to begin her university research, while teaching pre-service teachers at Macquarie University in educational psychology and science methodology. At the time of writing this chapter, she has now moved to coaching middle leaders, supporting them in working effectively with their new teachers to improve student outcomes.

In addition to teaching students, Steven has tutored and run workshops for new teachers at both Melbourne University and Victoria University, at the undergraduate and master's level, further developing his confidence with research and teaching across the age spectrum.

Online Activism and Representation

Stephy has been named among Australia's best teachers through the Commonwealth Bank/Australian Schools Plus Teaching Awards. She has appeared in the mainstream media as an example of teacher excellence, on ABC TV live and radio, as well as print media such as *The Sydney Morning Herald*, *The Daily Telegraph*, and the *Australian Teacher Magazine*. Feeling the weight of representing all Australian teachers, Stephy amplified the voice of her colleagues regarding the teacher shortage.

Steven was a top-50 finalist in the 2021 Global Teacher Prize and has appeared across major media platforms both as an interviewee and an author. He has been granted the opportunity to represent teachers' concerns globally through Education International's Future World of Work Committee and UNESCO's 'International Teacher Task Force on Teachers for Education 2030'. As a result, both Steven and Stephy are regularly contacted by teachers and leaders across Australia especially, but also the world, seeking advice and support.

Reflections

While desultory, cursory, and brief, we hope this short overview outlines outcomes that can emerge from this type of work, as a means of showing that this labour tends not to remain aspirational and unpaid. Noting that the steps outlined are completed in sequential fashion with the teacher developing their skills and voice across each phase.

OUR EXPERIENCES OF MIDDLE LEADERSHIP

The lack of leadership's support outlined above is largely a rhetorical device to draw in the possibilities and to highlight that all humans are flawed and fallible, no leader possesses all knowledge and all skill sets. This means that as developing or emerging middle leaders you have two options, seek outwards, new schools, and new contexts or stay and develop in the ways possible explored here. Indeed, looking at the areas of strengths that are present within your leadership team can mean you are able to source ways to contribute to this group or develop strengths in concert with them.

SEVEN STRONG CLAIMS ABOUT LEADERSHIP

Leithwood et al. (2008) noted and synthesised from the research literature seven strong claims about leadership; those most pertinent to this discussion are as follows:

> *Almost all successful leaders draw on the same repertoire of basic leadership practices.*
>
> *School leadership has a greater influence on schools and students when it is widely distributed. (p. 27)*

Claim 2 provides guidance in that leadership practices are relatively generic; this might sound disheartening, especially for those not given the opportunity or investment to practice and develop these skills. Yet, this is rather positive, as it means that through exploring online leadership and activism, aspirational leaders can be performing the same practices and tasks of other leaders within these spaces. Claim number 5 is important here because distribution is just what the practices and mindsets being cultivated by the approach outlined during this chapter seek, a wider distribution, indeed one not limited by the school gates but empowered by the wide web of the internet.

WHAT CAN BE DONE: OUR SEVEN STRONG CLAIMS OF DEVELOPING MIDDLE LEADERSHIP KNOWLEDGE AND SKILL SETS BEYOND YOUR SCHOOL

Mirroring the writing of Leithwood et al. (2008, 2020), we outline our own seven strong claims of how best to develop middle (and general) leadership knowledge and skill sets via online spaces, thereby providing a playbook for aspirational and emerging leaders to follow. More detailed and practically minded writing on our respective innovations that emerged from these processes can be accessed elsewhere (Kolber & Heggart, 2021, 2022; Kolber et al., 2021; Salazar, 2022). Fig. 6.2 represents our seven strong claims about how a middle leader can develop their leadership online.

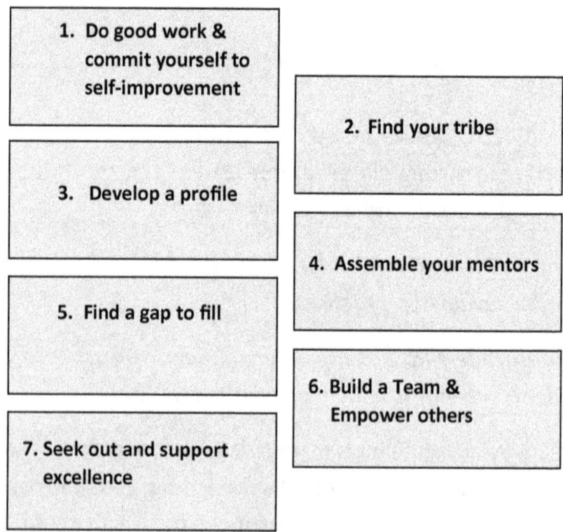

Fig. 6.2. The Authors' Seven Strong Claims About Personal Leadership Development Online.

Source: Authors' own creation.

DO GOOD WORK AND COMMIT YOURSELF TO SELF-IMPROVEMENT

The core thing you must establish is excellence in your work, developing your pedagogical strengths and gifts (Crowther & Boyne, 2016) to the level that they might be worth sharing. This is of course no small undertaking. The hardest work of all is internal work, no difficult conversation can ever rival the challenge of meeting oneself in internal conversation. The nature of this work is cyclical and rather trend sensitive. As a small illustration, Steven was among the global leaders in Flipped Learning in 2016, which was the emerging and exciting new pedagogical approach at that time. While for Stephy, her pedagogical and leadership skill as a young educator was her ability to transform research into practice as well as form deep, natural connections with other new teachers. This enabled her to work in partnership with colleagues to improve student growth through teacher growth. Thinking of your own work, consider what your pedagogical or leadership gift is, what is something that you have elevated above your colleagues in, think of the rather grounded question: What is a topic you could talk for an hour about with minimal preparation? It is likely that the answer to that question is your pedagogical or leadership gift.

FIND YOUR 'TRIBE'

The framing of 'finding your tribe' (Kolber & Enticott, 2020) is important here, considering the opening framing of this chapter, what can be done when your tribe is not geographically located within your school or workplace. Depending on the online platform that you are already most engaged with, think about how you might locate your work within those of other professions on that platform. Your tribe is colleagues and contemporaries, those with whom you would love to share a desk block with or a table within a virtual staffroom. Please note that we are not encouraging you to be in an echo chamber, that is, being in a space where your thinking remains static. It is important that your tribe consists of people who inspire you to be better, supportive of your growth and challenge you to think deeper and perhaps alternatively. Who is a leader you are inspired by? Who pushes you to be better and do better, even if your conversations make you squirm a little bit?

DEVELOP A PROFILE

Now that you have established your pedagogical gift, and found your tribe of colleagues, it is time to think of how best to share the former with the latter. The concept of 'developing a profile' may sound like a matter for influencers, but it is important and core work for leaders seeking to develop their own identity and strengths. The way to develop your profile, both in the sense of raw numbers of 'followers', etc., as well as the way in which this is clearly presented are both important. For us, this development can take the form of some of the other outputs outlined in section 'Self-Development and Reflection', including blogging, podcasting, and producing videos.

To help in the development of your profile, think about your vision for education. What is something that annoys you in education but also something you are willing to be part of solving? What *could* Australian education be? What difference would you like to make? For Stephy, part of her vision is that middle leaders understand how to ensure that new teachers feel supported, encouraged, and empowered, and consequently, more students experience intentional and impactful teaching. When you have spent the time to write, scribble, and rewrite your vision you should look at it and feel inspired and aligned personally and professionally. Use your vision to showcase yourself at school, within your school community and online, creating your bios on your social media platform. Try to align your online content to this as people will learn to associate you with certain areas/topics and then expect this from you in the future. You, being clear in your purpose, through your profile, will showcase your clarity, direction, and commitment as a leader. And that's what people want to follow!

ASSEMBLE YOUR MENTORS

Our personal experiences show that engaging with your tribe also tends to involve engaging with a more senior or experienced leader on the platform, to metaphorically 'show you the ropes'. This work takes the form of a digital mentoring that may circle around your pedagogical or leadership gift but will also include elements of more general mentoring around finding your voice and sharpening the quality of your outlooks.

Stephy is a big believer in always having coaches and mentors no matter what stage of career you are in. She continues to have leadership coaching sessions. Mentors may not know everything, but they may ask you some questions that surprise you, make you pause, and help you to find your own solutions. To find your mentors, ask yourself: Who inspires you in terms of the work that you want to do, at or beyond your school? What is it about them specifically that inspires you? How can you learn from them? Stephy is often asked how she is so connected to 'big names' in education and her response is: 'Just ask'. You'd be surprised who is willing to give up 30 minutes of their time to share their story with you. This has led to many fantastic collaborations between Stephy and other leaders in education. To Stephy, assembling mentors is like creating a fence of love and protection around yourself. No matter what happens on your journey, you will always have someone there to be with you and lift you up.

FIND A GAP TO FILL

The next necessary step is to look across the digital landscape of the platform that you have selected, as you have built your tribe and assembled your mentors you have effectively been completing this task. Who among the landscape is the most active, who is producing good work? Looking across these productions, which may take the form of groups, PL opportunities, webinars, writing, and podcasting, what is missing? Where is there a lack? And what should be the next steps. Just as school policies may seek to address needs or lacks within a school community, seeking a gap to fill is both a personal reflection of your own gifts and how these can best be contributed to the broader education community. This gap may mean the simple action of collecting people in real life (*IRL*) organising meetups and gatherings for your team or the broader, and newly formed, community.

BUILD A TEAM AND EMPOWER OTHERS!

As you are now part of a community, with a network of mentors, supporters, and perhaps even nemeses, you will need to build a team and empower those within the team or indeed those without it. This group can be put together to support your contribution to the community, promote one another's work and generally share in all the benefits of community. To make a clear school metaphor, this is your clique, *your people*, and provide all the benefits of that. With the added benefit of the fact that you can meet semi-regularly at conferences and similar gatherings.

SEEK OUT AND SUPPORT EXCELLENCE

The location and seeking of excellence, outlined within 'Finding your tribe' step is now bearing fruit and providing innumerable benefits to you and your peer group. But now, you are in the role of the elder statesperson that you were locating in the third phase of your process, where you sourced your mentors. You are the mentor, or at least a member of a productive and fruitful learning team or community, who can offer support and succour for those wandering untethered in the broader online spaces. It is now your task to outline these steps, either implicitly or explicitly and guide these new teachers into the powerful developments that have shaped you and your work.

TAKE ACTION NOW

To manifest your 'half glass full' viewpoint and generate your own agency in the absence of good leadership, a collegial school culture, and good PL you can take simple actions right now. We have listed five in Fig. 6.3. We also end this chapter with a couple of reflective questions that you may wish to respond to. Whatever it is you do, we emphasise that engaging in online leading, sharing, and collaborating is superb for developing cultural capital, improving your capability to influence, building an understanding of self, and refining upon areas for growth.

Action You Can Take Right Now

- Join subject associations and seek out board positions.
- Complete Ed Tech companies' accreditation to meet new middle leaders.
- Form a 'teacher-you' page on your preferred social media platform.
- Contact people you are inspired by and make connections.
- Find a coach/mentor you trust.

Fig. 6.3. Action You Can Take Right Now.

Source: Authors' own creation.

FURTHER REFLECTION QUESTIONS

1. What online social media platform do you have the most affinity with? Explore the features of this platform and identify ways you can engage more with platform.
2. What is your pedagogical gift? How can use share you gifts with others beyond your school?
3. Pick three references from the list at the end of this chapter and read them. What resonated with you? What might the ideas in this chapter mean for your leadership?

CONCLUSION

This chapter has outlined ways that online social mediated tools can be used in a bricolage approach to develop leadership and pedagogical gifts within oneself. In the absence of supportive leadership, or strong peer networks within one's schools, or indeed within a remote or rural situation, this approach is of great utility and importance. The personal vignettes outlined here have brought life to the taxonomy of steps involved in the process of this development. We, the authors, hope that the ideas outlined here do not seem too challenging to achieve and provide ways for you to conceptualise your own development as a leader within the online spaces. Depending upon your age and experience, you may well already be well along the path of developing your online leadership in this way, without ever conceiving of it as leadership development. If this is the case, do continue and, indeed, consider engaging with those contributions to the field outlined by the two authors also. We note the lack of strong practical support and policy approaches to developing middle leadership with the Australian system, unlike nations like Finland and Singapore (Berry et al., 2013; Kolber, 2022). While we believe that this work is incredibly important, in its absence, these approaches and practices have been nothing short of personally and professionally transformational.

REFERENCES

Barnes, N. (2021). How to value social media use in education. In J. S. Brooks & A. Heffernan (Eds.), *The school leadership survival guide: What to do when things go wrong, how to learn from mistakes, and why you should prepare for the worst* (pp. 155–168). IAP.

Benson, L. (2021). Middle leadership challenge: Leading to influence. *Australian Educational Leader*, *43*(3), 76–79.

Berry, B., Byrd, A., & Wieder, A. (2013). *Teacherpreneurs: Innovative teachers who lead but don't leave.* John Wiley & Sons.

Bressman, S., Winter, J. S., & Efron, S. E. (2018). Next generation mentoring: Supporting teachers beyond induction. *Teaching and Teacher Education*, *73*, 162–170.

Bryceson, T. (2012). TeachMeet: Sydney and beyond. *Scan: The Journal for Educators*, *31*(3), 48–51.

Campbell, C. (2022). Afterward? Moving onwards for developing pracademia and pracademics in education. *Journal of Professional Capital and Community*, *7*(1), 98–108.

Carpenter, J. P., & Harvey, S. (2019). "There's no referee on social media": Challenges in educator professional social media use. *Teaching and Teacher Education*, *86*, 102904.

Crowther, F., & Boyne, K. (2016). *Energising teaching: The power of your unique pedagogical gift.* ACER Press.

De Nobile, J. (2018). Towards a theoretical model of middle leadership in schools. *School Leadership & Management*, *38*(4), 395–416.

Dinham, S. (2016). *Leading learning and teaching*. ACER Press.

Duffy, B. E. (2017). *(Not) getting paid to do what you love: Gender, social media, and aspirational work*. Yale University Press.

Duignan, P. (2012). *Educational leadership: Together creating ethical learning environments*. Cambridge University Press.

Esterman, M. (2011). Meet a new kind of professional development: TeachMeet Sydney. *Teaching History*, *45*(3), 50–51.

Esterman, M. (2015). Changing education in action in Australia: The connected teacher. In J. Evers & R. Kneyber (Eds.), *Flip the system: Changing education from the ground up* (pp. 277–279). Routledge.

Grice, C. (2019). 007 Spies, surveillance and pedagogical middle leadership: For the good of the empire of education. *Journal of Educational Administration and History*, *51*(2), 165–181.

Heggart, K., & Kolber, S. (Eds.). (2022). *Empowering teachers and democratising schooling: Perspectives from Australia*. Springer Nature.

Kolber, J. (2022). Democracy starts in the classroom. In S. Kolber & K. Heggart (Eds.), *Empowering teachers and democratising schooling* (pp. 111–126). Springer.

Kolber, S. (2020). A new entrant into online professional learning offerings for teachers. *Professional Educator*, *23*(1), 55–57.

Kolber, S., & Heggart, K. (2021). Education focused pracademics on twitter: Building democratic fora. *Journal of Professional Capital and Community*, *7*(1), 26–44.

Kolber, S., & Heggart, K. (2022). Education focused pracademics on twitter: building democratic fora. *Journal of Professional Capital and Community*, *7*(1), 26–44.

Kolber, S., Nicoll, S., McGraw, K., Gaube, N., & Heggart, K. R. (2021). Leveraging social media and scholarly discussion for educator empowerment. *Australian Journal of Teacher Education (Online)*, *46*(11), 37–53.

Leithwood, K., Harris, A., & Hopkins, D. (2008). Seven strong claims about successful school leadership. *School Leadership and Management*, *28*(1), 27–42.

Leithwood, K., Harris, A., & Hopkins, D. (2020). Seven strong claims about successful school leadership revisited. *School Leadership & Management*, *40*(1), 5–22.

Mercieca, B. M. (2021). Sustaining online teacher networks. In B. M. Mercieca & J. McDonald (Eds.), *Sustaining communities of practice with early career teachers* (pp. 65–97). Springer. https://doi.org/10.1007/978-981-33-6354-0_4

Mercieca, B. M., & McDonald, J. (2021). *Sustaining communities of practice with early career teachers*. Springer.

Mockler, N. (2022). *Constructing teacher identities: How the print media define and represent teachers and their work*. Bloomsbury Publishing.

Nicoll, S. (2022). Empowering pre-service teachers: Perhaps being an influencer is a good thing? In K. Heggart & S. Kolber (Eds.), *Empowering teachers and democratising schooling: Perspectives from Australia* (pp. 223–237). Springer Nature.

Salazar, S. (2022). Welcome to the new teacher tribe: Empowering beginning teachers by co-creating sanctuaries of learning. In K. Heggart & S. Kolber (Eds.), *Empowering teachers and democratising schooling* (pp. 189–202). Springer.

Shine, K. (2018). Reporting education: How can we do it better? *Asia Pacific Media Educator*, *28*(2), 223–236.

Shine, K. (2020). 'Everything is negative': Schoolteachers' perceptions of news coverage of education. *Journalism*, 21(11), 1694–1709.

Southworth, G. (2008). Primary school leadership today and tomorrow. *School Leadership and Management*, *28*(5), 413–434.

West, R. (2022). The profession that eats itself: Addressing teacher infighting. In K. Heggart & S. Kolber (Eds.), *Empowering teachers and democratising schooling* (pp. 29–42). Springer.

Yallop, O. (2021). *Break the internet: In pursuit of influence*. Scribe Publications.

7

USING ACTION RESEARCH TO DRIVE TEACHER PROFESSIONAL LEARNING

Sarah Gunn[a] and Pamela Macklin[b]

[a]*St Peters Lutheran College Springfield, Springfield Central, QLD, Australia*
[b]*Zbar Consulting, St Kilda West, VIC, Australia*

ABSTRACT

Increasingly, schools are embracing action research as an innovative strategy to develop collective teacher efficacy and expertise in a bid to improve learner outcomes. In this chapter, what follows is an exploration of the challenges frequently faced by middle leaders implementing and facilitating action research in schools. These include low levels of collective autonomy, clouded evaluative thinking, and the siloing of success. To support middle leaders in overcoming these challenges, Sarah and Pamela offer an array of practical solutions they have witnessed working successfully in varying contexts. In doing so, they spotlight the work of educational thought leaders, Michael Fullan, Professor Emeritus Helen Timperley, Dr Kaye Twyford, and Simon Breakspear.

Keywords: Professional learning team; professional learning; action research; inquiry; middle leader; implementation

GUIDING QUESTIONS

The following are questions that you should ask yourself before you commence reading this chapter. The questions ask you to consider what you already know and feel about the topic.

1. How do you leverage context-specific problems of practice to spark professional curiosity and drive meaningful professional learning?
2. How do you build trust and a sense of shared purpose among your team?
3. How do you consciously craft opportunities for your team members' leadership to bloom and flourish?

ACTION RESEARCH: WHAT'S POSSIBLE?

Teacher professional learning matters. It matters because we know that effective teaching is what meaningfully impacts student learning outcomes in a positive way (Sahlberg, 2021). To deliver effective teaching – to be the best educators we can be – teachers at all career stages must commit to a cycle of ongoing professional renewal. Indeed, at the proficient level, Australian Institute for Teaching and School Leadership's (AITSL) Professional Standards for Teachers outline that educators are 'identifying and planning professional learning needs, engaging in professional learning and improving practice, engaging with colleagues and improving practice and applying professional learning and improving student learning' (AITSL, 2017). Clearly then, teacher professional learning is not a solo pursuit, nor an impractical endeavour of learning for learning's sake: its purpose is to engage with one another and contemporary research about what works, for whom and when to directly change the way we both understand and engage in practice for the immediate benefit of the learners in our care.

So, who in schools is ultimately responsible for leading the professional learning of teachers? Most often, it is middle leaders (Edwards-Groves et al., 2019). In this role, we occupy a space of duality. We are both expert and novice, leader and learner, master, and pupil. Michael Fullan (2011) refers to this responsibility as a *moral imperative* – it is our duty and privilege to be both the agent and beneficiary of school improvement. The good news is that there exists consensus in the literature about the features of effective professional learning that middle leaders can facilitate in schools. It is learning that is site based, ongoing, collaborative, autonomous, and supported.

One form of professional learning that fulfils these criteria is action research. Commonly, schools use professional learning teams (PLTs) to engage in action research. Here, PLTs will be defined as collaborative teams that 'engage in an ongoing cycle of decision making, implementation, evaluation and review in their use of data to enhance student learning outcomes' (Griffin et al., 2014, p. 130). In our view, action research – done well – is one of the most professionally fulfilling, rewarding, enlivening experiences that educators can embark upon together.

ACTION RESEARCH: PRACTICAL IMPLEMENTATION

For middle leaders seeking to facilitate action research in schools, there is no shortage of literature describing the features of impactful PLTs (Donohoo et al., 2018; Fullan & Pinchot, 2018; OECD, 2019). However, much of the literature is based in theory rather than practice or tends to focus on the process of PLT establishment (resourcing, vision-shaping, and momentum building) rather than the process of PLT inquiry. The practical *ongoing* implementation advice needed is often missing.

In an aim to make this chapter as useful a resource as possible to those leading improvement, Sarah asked middle leaders across schools in Brisbane, Queensland, Australia, this question: what are the biggest challenges you face in leading action research in your context? In synthesising their responses, Sarah has identified three of the most common problems that plague PLTs, causing them to become intractably 'stuck'. What follows is a description of these problems, an explanation of why they matter, and suggestions of how to tackle them.

CHALLENGE 1: COLLECTIVE AUTONOMY IS LOW

Why It Matters: Author Spotlight

International educational speaker, author, advisor, and researcher Andy Hargreaves is an advocate for a strong teacher profession enabled by collaborative professionalism. In his chapter 'Autonomy and Transparency: Two Good Ideas Gone Bad' (2019), Hargreaves criticises recent reforms that have transformed education into a neoliberal autocracy. He argues that unregulated school autonomy and top-down transparency do not achieve their aim of fostering higher educational standards in schools. In fact, Hargreaves contends they do the opposite, breeding incoherence, isolation, mistrust, and de-professionalisation. As an antidote, Hargreaves (2019) prescribes that schools pursue *collective autonomy*, which he defines as the 'constant communication and circulation of ideas in a coherent system where there is collective responsibility to achieve a common vision of student learning, development and success' (p. 12).

We argue that within PLTs, collective autonomy is evidenced by:

- A shared moral purpose among teachers, founded on the developmental belief that all students *can* learn and a valuing of equity in asserting that all students *deserve* to learn.
- A strong sense of collective efficacy, where educators are not only committed to every child's learning but also believe in their ability to cause learning as a direct result of their decisions and actions within the classroom.
- A collective feeling of belonging and relational trust in a non-threatening environment, where teachers feel safe to expose their practice, knowledge, and skills as they engage in the high-traction cost of collaborative inquiry to (re)form their professional identities.
- An empowerment of teachers as trusted adaptive experts through endeavours such as distributed leadership and shared decision making.

How to Diagnose It

When collective autonomy is low, teachers often are not invested in the work of PLT nor committed to one another's professional growth. Let us be clear: this isn't because teachers are apathetic. Typically, it occurs when teacher choice and/or voice is disregarded, shared purpose is not established, and/or leadership is concentrated.

So, how does one diagnose low collective autonomy? Common indicators include the following:

- Late arrival to and early departure from PLT meetings.
- Reluctance to engage in constructive or challenging professional dialogue.
- Preoccupation or multitasking during PLT meetings.
- A lack of professional investment in the PLT's inquiry focus.
- Forgetfulness in bringing agreed-upon materials or student work samples to PLT meetings.

How to Treat It

We suggest two key strategies that middle leaders facilitating PLTs can employ to cultivate collective autonomy.

Treatment 1: Empower Teachers As Leaders

Today, many PLTs around Australia are exclusively led by members of senior and middle leadership. A decision to isolate PLT leadership to those wielding formal leadership positions can have unintended negative consequences. Ultimately, it denies educators the opportunity to lead their own learning. One of the best ways in which we can leverage professional expertise to build professional capital (and foster trust) is to extend to our teachers the opportunity to lead and make decisions about PLTs. Of course, educators require time and support to do so. In one context Sarah worked in,

PLTs were led in even numbers by curriculum leaders and teachers. PLT learning leaders applied for the role in response to a detailed expression of interest issued by a PLT Steering Committee made up of diverse school representatives. This guiding coalition ensured that teacher voice informed PLT direction at both the strategic and operational levels.

In this context, all PLT learning leaders received support through ongoing professional development and resourcing, including training in action research models, data literacy skills, and leadership skills. PLT learning leaders met once a term as a group to engage in differentiated professional learning responsive to needs expressed throughout the year. They acted as critical friends for one another, sharing not only their wins but also seeking advice about how best to tackle barriers they faced. Further, Sarah created an all-access PLT NoteBook, which was stocked with resources to support PLT learning leaders, including sample meeting agendas, protocols, evidence articles, and impact measurement tools. For PLT learning leaders, this helped to build confidence, grow knowledge, and reduce planning time.

Treatment 2: Invest Time in Forming the Team

A second way that middle leaders can cultivate high levels of collective autonomy in PLTs is by investing valuable time in formation. Often, PLTs can be tempted to jump straight into the work of action research before having spent time building shared clarity about their purpose, values, beliefs, and behaviours. The measure of success for a PLT's first action research cycle is *not* necessarily impact on student learning in the first instance. Instead, success in the establishment phase of PLTs is evident when a PLT has embedded effective and efficient systems, protocols, and norms that enable its members to engage in the type of collaborative inquiry that moves learning forward.

A strategy that Sarah has seen successful PLTs utilise during their very first meeting to build shared clarity is engagement with Patrick Lencioni's (2012) six critical questions. There is great power in a PLT reflecting on and evolving their responses to these questions as their spirals of inquiry deepen learning over time. The questions are as follows:

1) Why do we exist?

This provocation calls PLTs to explicitly share their beliefs about education and the impact they hope to have in their collaborative inquiry.

2) How do we behave?

This provocation calls PLTs to decide what behavioural norms and language choices will define their interaction. Examples – 'no place for blame, shame or fame', 'evidence over inference', and '*our* students, not *my* students'. Clear behavioural protocols reduce ambiguity, encourage risk-taking, and foster trust.

3) What do we do?

This provocation calls PLTs to decide what inquiry model will scaffold their action research, what the focus of their inquiry cycle might be, and justify this need based on evidence or strategic priorities. Example:

> *We will use a Teaching Sprint to investigate Spaced Practice because our Year 12 Maths students have self-reported a lack of confidence in preparing for their 50% external exam (supported by an emerging historic trend of stronger achievement on internal than external assessment).*

When teachers are empowered to make these decisions freely, their commitment to the work of the PLT is instantly enhanced because they see it as purposeful.

4) How will we succeed?

This provocation calls PLTs to define what success looks like in each action inquiry cycle. For example – a first-time PLT might define success as having consistently honoured the norms they co-developed, brought student work samples to each meeting, and produced milestone artefacts at each stage of their inquiry cycle.

5) What is most important, right now?

This provocation calls PLTs to consider and communicate what they need to operate as an effective team. This might involve specific professional learning needs, access to research, or an online space to collect and analyse evidence. Senior and middle leaders are encouraged to understand and action the needs of PLTs if enthusiasm and commitment is to be sustained.

6) Who must do what?

This provocation calls PLTs to decide how they will make use of their time together, including what they will and will not tolerate. For example, PLTs might decide to rotate key roles, such as that of Norms Monitor, Decision Recorder, and Meeting Facilitator. These decisions increase lateral accountability.

CHALLENGE 2: EVALUATIVE THINKING IS CLOUDED

Why It Matters: Author Spotlight

In a two-part article recently published in *Australian Educational Leader* (AEL), Professor Emeritus Helen Timperley and Dr Kaye Twyford (2022) explore the concept of adaptive expertise. They contend that routine expertise – the expertise relied upon to solve simple, technical, or predictable problems – is not sufficient to effectively respond to the complex problems educators face today. In today's context, argue Timperley and Twyford, educators require adaptive expertise to successfully design sustainable, scalable, impactful change. Adaptive expertise is a new way of thinking and acting. In employing adaptive expertise, educators tolerate ambiguity comfortably, interrogate assumptions critically, and deepen knowledge collaboratively. Timperley and Twyford put forward six attributes of adaptive expertise in educational leadership. In our opinion, the most critical of these attributes is the ability to think and act evaluatively. When a team of educators, such as a PLT, think and act evaluatively, they are curious about learner experience, consider diverse perspectives, are aware of personal bias, use evidence critically, and measure learner impact. An example of a PLT timeline is provided in Table 7.1.

Table 7.1. PLT Timeline.

Stage	Weeks	Evaluative Thinking and Action
Introductory meeting	Week 1	Agreeing upon purpose
Scan: what is going on for learners?	Week 2	Seeking and understanding diverse perspectives
Focus: what will have the biggest impact?	Week 3	Making an evaluative judgement
Develop a hunch: how are we contributing to the situation?	Week 4	Acknowledging biases and assumptions to engage in problem solving
Learn: what do we need to learn and how will we learn this?	Weeks 5 and 6	Committing to collaborative learning and dialogue
Act: what can we do that will make a meaningful difference?	Weeks 7–9	Deciding upon responsive, shared actions, and capturing evidence of impact
Check: have we made enough of a difference? How do we know?	Week 10	Analysing challenging evidence to measure impact and consider various interpretations

How to Diagnose It

When evaluative thinking is clouded, PLTs (often time or resource poor) frame complex problems as simple or technical ones. Swift judgements are made about a problem of practice's contributing causes, thereby leading to an incorrect diagnosis. When this occurs, PLTs often select poorly matched, unreliable treatments, which inevitably lead to 'patchy' impact on learner outcomes.

So, how does one diagnose clouded evaluative thinking? Common indicators include the following:

- a reliance upon narrow, inconclusive, or unreliable forms of evidence;
- a tendency to draw fast conclusions from data and act hastily;
- superficial professional dialogue, where PLT members feel discomforted by disagreement or ambiguity; and
- a fascination with and pursuit of popular or 'new' high-impact strategies.

How to Treat It

To sharpen evaluative thinking and actions within a PLT, we believe that middle leaders must pay careful attention to the way in which they structure the pace and focus of their PLT inquiry cycle. In doing so, middle leaders can intentionally design opportunities for their team to practice evaluative thinking and action. What follows are three such opportunities.

Treatment 1: Map a PLT Timeline

All inquiry cycles follow a clear process, regardless of their varying levels of complexity. What some middle leaders report difficulty in deciding is how long to spend in each stage of inquiry. In considering momentum, middle leaders must ensure they leave enough time for their team to engage in deep evaluative thinking but not so much time that the team becomes 'bogged down' without action. In Table 7.1, a sample timeline for a term-long Spiral of Inquiry is shown. It assumes that the PLT meets once per week. The Spiral of Inquiry (Timperley, 2020) is a model that provokes evaluative thinking and action at each stage. Sarah recommends that a PLT decides upon their inquiry cycle timeline in Meeting 1. Not only does this promote collective autonomy but so too does it clarify the direction and purpose of the PLT.

Treatment 2: Spend Time Rewiring Mental Models

Every educator has a complex tangle of values, attitudes, beliefs, biases, and assumptions that shape our professional identity. These mental models are important because they help us to make sense of the world; they guide our perceptions and our behaviour. Often, our mental models are invisible to us. These blind spots can cloud evaluative thought and action, causing PLT members to misinterpret information or make poor decisions. The most effective of PLTs sharpen evaluative thought and action by utilising metacognitive protocols that help them to think reflectively and act with self-awareness. Some examples follow:

A. *The Ladder of Inference* (Senge, 2006) (Fig. 7.1) is a mental model that helps people visualise what happens in their minds as they select data, interpret it, draw conclusions, and act. Sarah shares this tool early in the PLT inquiry cycle so that team members can remind one another 'not to run up the ladder too quickly' when analysing and interpreting evidence for decision making.

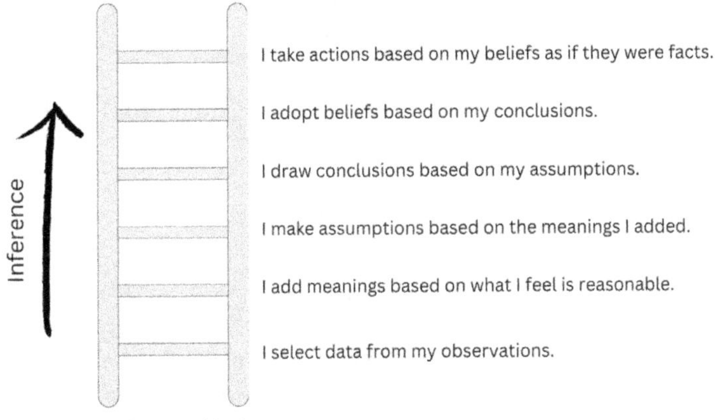

Fig. 7.1. Ladder of Inference.
Source: Adapted from Senge (2006).

B. The *ATLAS Looking at Data* protocol (School Reform Initiative, 2023) supports PLT members to transform data into insightful knowledge for action. Educators spend 10 minutes reviewing student work silently, then 30 minutes round-robin style describing noticings, sharing wonderings, suggesting implications, and selecting next steps for classroom practice.

CHALLENGE 3: SUCCESS IS SILOED

Why It Matters: Author Spotlight

Dr Simon Breakspear, Visiting Fellow at the Gonski Institute for Education, researches and advises on educational leadership through evidence-based change. Like Timperley and Twyford,

Breakspear (2017) recognises that educators are working in a Rapid, Unpredictable, Paradoxical, and Tangled (RUPT) context where complexities are often overlooked, leading to teacher frustration and fatigue. It is in this context that Breakspear (2017) makes the case for embracing an 'agile change process' (p. 70) as a way of de-risking change and ensuring impactful scalability. The process involves three stages:

- Phase 1 – Clarify. Pursing less but better.
- Phase 2 – Incubate. Searching for solutions.
- Phase 3 – Amplify. Get more of what is working (2017, p. 70).

In designing a considered, lengthy amplification timeline over 6–18 months, Breakspear (2017) argues there is a far greater likelihood of those strategies deemed to be most successful being noticed, understood, and adopted. The amplification stage is what disrupts the siloed success we see so often in our schools. Breakspear (2017) encourages leaders to move slowly during this stage, thoughtfully curating collaborative learning experiences that enable teams to shift habits and routines.

How to Diagnose It

When success is siloed, educators and PLTs are unaware of the wins of other educators in their context. Each PLT toils in isolation, working to tackle problems of practice that other PLTs may very well possess the keys to unlocking. The morale and motivation of teachers and middle leaders dip, as the fruits of PLT labours are seemingly out of reach.

So, how does one diagnose siloed success? Common indicators include:

- there exists no lateral structure for PLT leaders to share progress, challenges, and ideas with one another as critical friends or mentors;
- there is a lack of whole-school events for PLTs to report their results of their inquiry with colleagues;

- there is no system for successful PLT teaching strategies to be formalised through addition to whole-school policy; and
- Senior leaders do not regularly publicly acknowledge and celebrate the success of PLTs.

How to Treat It

We know that much of the expertise educators require to thrive already exists in the four walls of the school. What we need to do better in schools is to create an environment that enables such knowledge to be shared. We believe that middle leaders play a critical role in designing this environment as they are much closer to 'the action' than senior leaders and are well placed to nurture a healthy professional learning culture that grows collective autonomy and adaptive expertise. Here, we suggest several strategies that can be employed to celebrate success.

Treatment 1: Showcase Events

In schools where Sarah and Pamela have worked, PLT Showcase events are held each semester or annually. These events contribute to the development of a learning culture that values curiosity, risk-taking, and professional collaboration. They can take a variety of forms but always include the strong presence of senior leaders who affirm and celebrate the work of PLTs, along with the sharing of successes and challenges via presentations in various forms, including videos, data, and student work. One school Sarah worked in used the questions in Table 7.2 to prompt learning conversations during a PLT Showcase event.

Treatment 2: Sharing Classroom Practice – Lesson Observations, Videos, and Podcasts

One of the best ways to amplify success and support teachers in adopting proven classroom teaching strategies is to invest in professional observation. Myriad lesson observation strategies exist, of varying complexity and resource intensity. Given the heavy

Table 7.2. Questions to Prompt Learning Conversations.

Q1. What is one thing that surprised you when looking at data or evidence during your PLT meetings?	Q2. If you could change one thing about how your PLT ran, what would it look like?
Q3. What is one thing that you really admire about one of your colleague's teaching that you wish you could do?	Q4. What is one thing you contributed to your peers' learning during your PLT meetings?
Q5. Of all your PLT accomplishments this year, what is one thing you learned that you would want a teacher working on the year level above or below you to know?	Q6. Who are the external experts in education that you look up to and why?
Q7. What PLT actions are we better at now when compared to Term 1?	Q8. Where to next? What problem are you curious to investigate in your next PLT inquiry cycle?

Source: Authors' own creation.

demands on time and other resources required to conduct effective lesson observations, Pamela is seeing many schools increasingly support teachers to use video recordings to share, analyse, and improve practice. The work of Dr Jim Knight (2014) has been instrumental in providing a range of structures, processes, and tools to support instructional practice improvement in a way that builds collaboration and amplifies successful practice, often using video as key evidence for reflective practice.

Additionally, Sarah is noticing schools utilise podcast creation as an in-house professional learning strategy. To share site-specific success with other teachers, PLTs can record a podcast episode (including images and text) that explain – step by step – how to implement a proven successful teaching strategy within context, including pitfalls to avoid and resources to utilise. Of course, schools are encouraged to provide teachers with time to engage with the podcast bank in alignment with personal learning plans and pedagogical frameworks, perhaps even as part of an ongoing induction process.

FINAL THOUGHTS

Importantly, there is too little attention paid to how we can ensure that school leaders at all levels understand the key factors necessary to establish, implement, and embed effective PLTs in a way that is sustainable in the long term. Schools are dynamic systems. As staff, priorities and resources change over time, the sustaining factors for whole-school PLT effectiveness can wane without careful attention. For example, is there a clear process for new staff to be supported to understand the why, what, and how of PLTs in the school context? Or do we just assume that new colleagues will learn by participation and osmosis? How can we be confident that there is consistent implementation of PLTs over time? Are we regularly monitoring, reviewing, and adjusting how we are working in PLTs and how effective they are? Is the time for PLT work privileged and prioritised? It is important that middle leaders ask – and answer – these questions if we are to be truly successful in leading learning and leading change.

REFERENCES

Australian Institute for Teaching and School Leadership (AITSL). (2017). *Australian Professional Standards for Teachers*. https://www.aitsl.edu.au/standards

Breakspear, S. (2017). Embracing agile leadership for learning: How leaders can create impact despite growing complexity. *Australian Educational Leader*, *39*(3), 68–71. https://search.informit.org/doi/10.3316/aeipt.219755

Donohoo, J., Hattie, J., & Eells, R. (2018). The power of collective efficacy. *Educational Leadership: Journal of the Department of Supervision and Curriculum Development, N.E.A.*, *75*(6), 40–44.

Edwards-Groves, C., Grootenboer, P., Hardy, I., & Rönnerman, K. (2019). Driving change from 'the middle': Middle leading for site based educational development. *School Leadership & Management*, *39*(3–4), 315–333. https://doi.org/10.1080/13632434.2018.1525700

Fullan, M., & Ontario Principals' Council. (2011). *The moral imperative realized*. Corwin Press.

Fullan, M., & Pinchot, M. (2018). The fast track to sustainable turnaround. *Educational Leadership*, *75*(6), 48–54.

Griffin, P., Care, E., Crigan, J., Robertson, P., Zhang, Z., & Arratia-Martinez, A. (2014). The influence of evidence-based decisions by collaborative teacher teams on student achievement. In S. Billett, C. Harteis, & H. Gruber (Eds.), *International handbook of research in professional and practice-based learning* (p. 130). Springer.

Hargreaves, A. (2019). Autonomy and transparency: Two good ideas gone bad. In D. M. Netolicky, J. Andrews, & C. Paterson (Eds.), *Flip the system Australia: What matters in education* (p. 12). Routledge.

Knight, J. (2014). *Focus on teaching using video for high-impact instruction.* Corwin Press.

Lencioni, P. (2012). *The advantage: Why organizational health trumps everything else in business.* John Wiley & Sons.

OECD. (2019). *TALIS 2018 results: Teachers and school leaders as lifelong learners.* OECD Publishing.

Sahlberg, P. (2021). *Finnish lessons 3.0: What can the world learn from educational change in Finland?* (3rd ed.). Teachers College Press, Columbia University.

School Reform Initiative. (2023). *Atlas – Learning from student work protocol.* https://www.schoolreforminitiative.org/download/atlas-learning-from-student-work-protocol/

Senge, P. M. (2006). *The fifth discipline: The art and practice of the learning organization* (Revised and updated ed.). Random House Business.

Timperley, H. (2020). *Leading professional learning: Practical strategies for impact in schools.* ACER Press.

Timperley, H., & Twyford, K. (2022). Building a learning culture through the attributes of adaptive expertise. *The Australian Educational Leader*, *44*(2), 8–16.

LEADING LEARNING AND LEADING CHANGE FOR IMPROVEMENT

8

MIDDLE LEADERS: STRATEGIC THINKERS AND STRATEGIC PLANNERS

Elizabeth Benson[a]

[a]*Pivotal Leadership, Gold Coast, QLD, Australia*

ABSTRACT

As the role of senior school leaders has become more complex, the leadership of improvement, innovation and change has been distributed to middle leaders. However, middle leaders are often not prepared for the shift to strategic thinking and leading. This chapter provides an overview of what it means to think and lead strategically when leading from the middle. Then, the theory is translated into practical templates and tools that can be employed by a middle leader. The context of this chapter is leading a faculty in a secondary school; however, the ideas and examples provided are easily translated to any middle leading context.

Keywords: Strategic thinking; strategic planning; strategic capability; school improvement; goals; action planning

GUIDING QUESTIONS

The following are questions that you should ask yourself before you commence reading this chapter. The questions ask you to consider what you already know and feel about the topic.

1. Take 10 minutes to write a list of the tasks you undertake in your day and week. Which tasks require you to tap into your strategic thinking?
2. Who do you collaborate with when establishing strategic plans for your team or faculty? What does the collaboration look, feel and sound like?

HAS THE ROLE OF A MIDDLE LEADER BECOME MORE ABOUT LEADING SCHOOL IMPROVEMENT THAN MANAGING TEXTBOOKS AND MEETINGS?

I'm not sure exactly when my role as a middle leader changed from managing textbooks and excursions to leading school improvement. But I do know that the biggest single change to my middle leadership practice has been the transformation from 'managing' the curriculum, teachers and students to 'leading' improvement, innovation and change. As the role of senior school leaders has become more complex, the leadership of improvement, innovation and change has been distributed (or delegated) to heads of department, leading teachers, team leaders and other middle leaders (Harvey & Beauchamp, 2005).

This evolution in the work of middle leaders is significant. The Queensland Department of Education states that the 'strategic school leadership, is leading school improvement' (2022, p. 1) and the NSW Department of Education declares: 'School improvement is at the heart of the work we do as teachers and school leaders, and needs to "touch every classroom", be the work of every teacher and impact every student' (NSW Department of Education, 2021)

It appears that middle leaders are the bridge between school strategic goal implementation and student learning (Grootenboer et al., 2020). The work of middle leaders has become more complex and focused on school improvement (Bryant, 2018). Adam Robbins

(2021, p. 1) suggests in his book, *Middle Leadership Mastery*, that 'there is a greater appreciation for the role of subject specialists in making decisions about the strategic direction of each department'.

I will argue that middle leaders are key drivers and implementers of school improvement strategy, and therefore, strategic leadership skills are now essential to the leading work of middle leaders. As the New Zealand Ministry of Education asserts, educators leading from the middle have 'a pivotal part to play in helping their schools pursue their goals and achieve their objectives' (Ministry of Education, 2012, p. 11).

The Australian Professional Standard for Principals and associated Leadership Profiles (Australian Institute for Teaching and School Leadership, 2017) provide principals with guidance on what leading improvement, innovation and change looks like. Interestingly, if the terms *Principal* and *School* are replaced with *Middle Leader* and *Faculty* in the standard document, improvement, innovation and change would read as follows:

> ***Middle Leaders*** *identify the need for innovation and improvement that is consistent with the* ***faculty*** *vision and values and is informed by student learning outcomes. They communicate the need for change to the* ***faculty*** *community in an inspirational and logical way. They deepen their own knowledge and understanding of improvement strategies, leading change, and innovation at a whole* ***faculty level.*** *They engage and inspire staff to commit to evidence-based improvement, change and innovation that has a positive impact on student learning.*

This description reflects the nature of my middle leadership work for the last 15 years, and I would argue it reflects the work of many middle leaders.

The challenge for education right now is that while the work of middle leaders has changed, there has been little guidance for middle leaders on how to lead improvement, innovation and change. Authors, researchers, systems, consultants and schools have yet to catch up and provide middle leaders with professional learning that reflects the unique nature of leading strategically for school improvement, innovation and change from the middle.

The growing importance of middle leaders to school improvement requires them to draw on an expanding repertoire of leadership skills (Crane & De Nobile, 2014, in Bryant, 2018). Davies and Davies (2006) argue that leaders need to develop their ability to lead strategically. I believe that I have done just this, and this chapter will provide insights into what I have learnt about thinking and leading strategically for improvement, innovation and change in a faculty. Like a bowerbird, I am a collector of strategic planning tools and templates, and over time, I have tried and adapted them into a strategic thinking flow, an action planning template, with reflection questions to guide strategic thinking.

WHAT DOES IT MEAN TO LEAD STRATEGICALLY FROM THE MIDDLE?

Leading from the middle is different from leading as a principal (Grootenboer et al., 2020). I believe the difference is in the limited power of middle leaders to make strategic decisions with autonomy and access to resources. As such, leading strategically from the middle requires highly tuned influence skills to generate support for faculty strategic direction and plans from both senior leadership and teachers. The ability to influence is determined by the clarity of the leader's thinking, planning and communication.

Davies and Davies (2006) state that strategic leadership is a key dimension of any leadership activity. According to the Collins (2022) dictionary, to be strategic means to be tactical, calculated, deliberate and planned. Middle leaders often state that being calculated, deliberate and planned (or leading strategically) is a challenge because of their constant shift from operational to strategic cognition. Today, many heads of departments are seeking training in strategic leadership. In their research Boyle et al. (2002) found that the heads of departments they interviewed identified the need to develop strategic planning skills. Key areas of need identified are the ability to:

- think and plan in short, medium and long terms;
- relate subject/department aims to the wider school goals;
- implement corporate planning at the subject level; and
- prioritise of objectives.

WHAT DO STRATEGIC LEADERS DO?

Davies and Davies' (2006) research found that strategic leaders involve themselves in five key activities to translate their strategies into action:

1. Direction setting.
2. Translating strategy into action.
3. Enabling staff to develop and deliver the strategy.
4. Determining effective intervention points.
5. Developing strategic capabilities.

In the rest of this chapter, I will explore strategies and tools middle leaders can use to set a faculty direction and translate their strategies into action. For me, strategic planning when leading from the middle can be defined as the leadership activities a middle leader engages in to lead in a planned and deliberate manner to set, implement and achieve faculty and school improvement goals. Strategy and strategic planning are different:

> **Strategy** is '... a way of intentionally thinking and acting by giving sense to a specific school (faculty) vision or mission' (Carvalho et al., 2021, p. 2), and
> **Strategic planning** is the act of turning the strategy into action – I call this *action planning*. However, action planning encompasses more than identifying goals, actions, resources and timelines.

DEVELOPING STRATEGIC CAPABILITY

Thinking and planning strategically requires a middle leader to have strategic intelligence. According to Davies and Davies (2006), strategic intelligence is made up of people, contextual and procedural wisdom (p. 134). For example, when developing action plans for a faculty, a middle leader must consider the skills and knowledge needed by teachers to implement the actions. They must also be clear about who they should collaborate with to generate commitment to implementing the plans. This is the **people wisdom** of strategic intelligence. Middle leaders must also consider the **context** within which their strategic leadership takes place. The work of a middle leader is not 'unidimensional' and is a part of a '... multifaceted, overlapping complex of other practices to education' (Grootenboer et al., 2020, pp. 19–21) therefore, middle leaders must be sensitive to: 'understanding and developing culture; sharing values and beliefs; developing networks and understanding the external environment' (Davies & Davies, 2006, p. 136). Davies and Davies (2006) make a clear connection between the work of teachers in classrooms, achievement of faculty goals, school strategic goals and ultimately contributing to the broader education system goals.

Finally, **procedural wisdom** focuses on the 'strategic learning cycle that enables the appropriate choice of strategic approach and appropriate choice of strategic processes'. They claim that in their experience, a collaborative action research approach, founded in an appreciative inquiry mindset, has enabled them to 'harness the abilities of others' (Davies & Davies, 2006, p. 136) and have the courage to work with their team to lead improvement in their faculty.

DIRECTION SETTING

Identifying and setting the strategic direction for a faculty starts by tapping into contextual wisdom and scanning the environment for broader school and system goals and the needs of students and teachers. Fig. 8.1 represents how I see the flow of strategic thinking when leading from the middle.

Before goals and actions can be established for the faculty, I always identify the system and school goals and measures of impact. I make sure those goals are documented at the start of any action plans (see Table 8.2). Then, using evidence, I collaborate with my team and colleagues to determine the goals for the faculty. Importantly, we establish three-year and one-year goals and measures. Involving my team in these processes ensures that when they then determine improvement goals for their subject or professional learning teams, they are fully committed to the faculty goals.

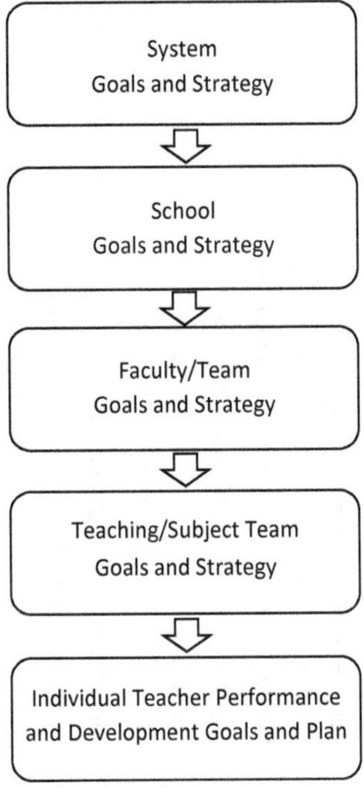

Fig. 8.1. Strategic Planning Flow Chart for Middle Leaders.

Source: Author's own creation.

And finally, the information from the first four phases of planning informs the performance and development goals that individual teachers set for their own development.

Table 8.1 unpacks each of these phases further by providing the middle leader with questions that they can use to reflect on their strategic thinking and planning. Use the reflection activity below to reflect on your current strategic thinking and planning.

REFLECTION ACTIVITY

Before you begin, you will need a copy of your current strategic planning for your faculty, as well as your school and system strategic plans. You will also need highlighters and pens. I encourage you to collaborate on this activity with members of your team. Carefully examine your faculty planning documents by responding to each

Table 8.1. Questions for Reflecting on Faculty Strategic Planning.

Level	Description	Reflection Questions
System	Contextual wisdom requires that the middle leaders identify not only the school's improvement goals but also the goals of the broader system. It is from these goals that the school leadership team determines the school's strategic goals for the year	Examine your current faculty strategic plan: • Highlight where you see system goals and language • Highlight where you have referenced system policy/frameworks/tools/resources in your planning • What do you notice about the alignment between your faculty plans and the broader system goals and language?
School	Before any strategic planning can occur at the faculty level, a middle leader must be aware of the school strategic plan. Identifying the relevant school strategic goals (and measures) will ensure that the efforts of faculty members will contribute to the achievement of school goals. It is also important to identify relevant evidence sets that have guided the creation of school goals	Examine your current faculty strategic plan: • Which goals of the whole school strategic plan does your faculty plan aim to support the achievement of? • Can a clear line of sight be drawn between your faculty goals and specific whole school goals? • Where do you see misalignment between your faculty goals and the whole school goals? • How have you fed the development/learning needs of the teachers and students in your faculty to the whole school strategic plan? • Can a clear line of sight be drawn between the evidence sets used to determine the impact of faculty goal achievement and whole school goal achievement?

Faculty	A faculty strategic plan is written documentation of your strategic thinking and proposed actions. It includes information that communicates: Strategic vision for the faculty Alignment of the faculty goals to system and school goals Clear improvement goals Planned actions to achieve the goals Evidence of impact measures Professional learning required to enact the planned actions Human/physical/financial resources needed to enact the planned actions And strategies for collaboratively developing and implementing the faculty visions and action plan	Examine your current faculty strategic plan: • Do you have a long-term plan (3–5 years) for your faculty? • Who do you collaborate with when planning at this level? Who else might you need to collaborate with? • What goals/targets in your plan support the achievement of school goals/targets? • Where have you utilised data/evidence from the school data plan in your plan? • How you identified the quantitative and qualitative evidence you will use to measure the impact? • Have you identified the skills/knowledge required of teachers and leaders to successfully implement the actions? • Have you identified the relevant professional learning to successfully implement the actions? • Does your action plan include human/physical/financial resources needed for successful implementation? • Does each goal have clear success criteria and identified evidence of success? • Have you identified colleagues who you need to collaborate, communicate and/or consult with?

(*continued*)

Table 8.1. ***(Continued)***

Level	Description	Reflection Questions
Team, for example, subject team	Each faculty consists of teaching or subject teams. Using the faculty and school goals as their starting point, each team needs clear goals for student learning and an action plan for achieving these goals. In many schools, this may occur in professional learning teams. The goals and actions of these teams should be documented in the faculty strategic plan	Examine your current faculty strategic plan: • Are your teams/groups of teachers/students identified in your planning? • Where have you identified goals and measures? • Where have you detailed the actions team members need to take? • Have you identified the professional learning individuals or teams might need to achieve the goals? • Where in your plan is it clear the connection between your team plans and the faculty/school/system goals? • Who did you collaborate with in developing the plan? Who might you need to collaborate with?

Individual	To build capability and embed accountability teachers engage in annual performance and development planning. These plans encourage teachers to set individual performance and development goals aligned to the goals of their subject teams, faculty and school. They also allow for career and interest goal setting	Examine your current faculty strategic plan: • Where are the phases of the performance/development process reflected in your current plans? • What do your capability development conversations look, feel and sound like? • How confident/comfortable are you with the performance/development conversations you lead? • Do your team members have a clear understanding of and commitment to faculty plans so that they can align their performance and development goals to faculty goals? • Who do you collaborate with in planning for and implementing the performance/development process? Who might you need to collaborate with?

Source: Author's own creation.

question in the third column of Table 8.1, annotating your plans as you go. After thorough reflection, respond to these two questions:

1. What are the strengths of your strategic planning processes?
2. What changes might you need to make to your planning processes?

TRANSLATING STRATEGY INTO ACTION

When it comes to developing plans, strategic planning templates can be useful to guide thinking and encourage the middle leaders to document their plans. Written plans should be viewed as evolving, live documents that are an essential communication tool for the middle leader.

Two templates that I have created to fuel my planning are:

- The strategic planning template for middle school leaders.
- The action planning template for middle school leaders.

Template 1: Strategic Planning Template

The Strategic Planning Template (see Table 8.2) for middle leaders summarises the cascading goals and measures of impact a middle

Table 8.2. Template 1: Strategic Planning Template for School Middle Leaders.

Level of Planning	Goals	Measures of Impact
System goals		
School long-term planning cycle (3–5 years)		
School annual goals		
Faculty long-term goals (3–5 years)		
Faculty annual goals		

Source: Author's own creation.

leader needs to consider when thinking strategically. The idea is that the middle leader sifts through the goals and associated measures at the system and school level, then chooses the relevant goals that their faculty can contribute to and, finally, documents both the goals and the measures.

The middle leader can then use informing evidence to set relevant and aligned goals for their faculty and measures of impact. It is important to summarise this information at the start of any action planning as it reminds the middle leaders of the context they are working within.

Template 2: Action Planning Template

The second and most important template (see Table 8.3) clarifies exactly what the middle leader (and their team) will do to achieve the faculty goals. The Action Planning Template for middle leaders is a comprehensive action planning template that has been developed over my 20+ years of leading school improvement. While this template has many columns, I feel it provides a good summary of the strategic thinking behind the goals and planned actions to achieve the goals. I encourage you to choose and adapt the columns that suit your leadership practice and school context.

- *Current reality*: A description of what is currently happening in the focus area, including any learning data, culture factors, human/physical/financial resource issues.
- *Improvement goals*: Specific goals to improve on the current reality. These goals can be written with a SMART frame.
- *Success criteria*: A description of what success would look like. Success can be described for each group of stakeholders.
- *Evidence of progress*: Consider both qualitative and quantitative evidence. Identify monitoring and review points in time and evidence.
- *Actions*: List the actions that are needed to be taken and by whom.
- *Who will you collaborate with?* Identify individuals and teams that you need to collaborate with to ensure plans are well

Table 8.3. Template 2: Action Planning Template for School Middle Leaders.

Current Reality	Goals	Success Criteria	Evidence of Progress	Actions	Who Will You Collaborate With? Consult? Inform?	Connection to System, School Goals, Policies, Frameworks, etc.
Example: Leaders' ability to lead moderation cycles is in the foundation stages for 3 out of 10 new HODs	Influence the development of leader skills to use the moderation cycle as a vehicle for developing culture, curriculum and pedagogical knowledge and skills	All HODs' self-reflections about their ability to and confidence in leading the implementation of the moderation cycle are in the knowledge or action phase	Leader self-reflection on behaviour change (AITSL, 2017) model in Term 3 Week 9 and Term 4 Week 7	Develop and implement a professional learning course to build leaders ability to develop culture/curriculum/pedagogy through moderation	Director of curriculum Deputy principal curriculum HODs	Professional Learning Teams (PLTs) System moderation policy, process, and tools Australian curriculum Queensland Curriculum and Assessment Authority (QCAA) syllabus

HODs, heads of department.
Source: Author's own creation.

informed and there is commitment by relevant stakeholders to support the implementation.

- *Connection to system, school goals, policies, frameworks*: Identify the relevant system and school goals, policies and frameworks that support or inform your faculty strategic plans.

A key barrier to successful implementation of faculty improvement plans and goal achievement is lack of ownership by the teachers who implement the actions in the classroom. Commitment to working together to achieve goals emerges from being involved in goal setting and action planning to achieve the goals. Middle leaders cannot strategically plan on their own, with their office door shut. They must collaborate with the teachers in their teams, other middle leaders, their line manager and their school principal. Harvey and Beauchamp (2005) states that 'collaboration and collegial working are crucial influences on school improvement' and are a 'feature of successful departments' (p. 63). Leading strategically also involves finding ways to enable staff to develop and deliver the strategy (Davies & Davies, 2006).

This may seem very time-consuming, but in my experience, it is much easier to influence people and garner their commitment when they have been involved in the thinking and planning. Traditionally, strategic plans are communicated to those who need to implement them once they have been developed. The objectives of such communication are to build shared understanding, commitment and ownership. A middle leader who collaborates with stakeholders during the strategic thinking and planning process enhances the clarity of communication and therefore has a greater chance that plans will be implemented as intended and improvement goals achieved.

BUT I DON'T HAVE TIME TO LEAD STRATEGICALLY!

The other challenge for middle leaders is to prioritise their strategic thinking and planning. In all contexts within which I have led a faculty, this has probably been my biggest frustration. Wanting to support teachers and students' day-to-day, while taking actions to improve long-term learning opportunities for students. While there is no magic bullet, and I could suggest middle leaders dedicate one hour every week to strategic thinking and planning, I know that such routines are hard to sustain in a school. However, I agree with Bendkison (2019) that leaders need to work 'cleverly with and through the skill of others'. Not only does collaborating with colleagues help with clarifying thinking and securing commitment, for me it also provides a level of accountability to put aside the time to strategically think and plan.

I also appreciate the advice of Adam Robbins (2021) when he suggests that middle leaders can consider what needs to be implemented to 100% and what might need less. Adam's advice is sound. When deciding on an improvement goal and associated actions, also agree on the level to which that goal needs to be implemented and achieved. Some goals are just as effective when implemented to 80% as they are 100%. There is a resource opportunity cost (time, energy, cognitive load, money, etc.) when actions are taken that push implementation beyond what is needed for effectiveness. This opportunity cost is a useful consideration when prioritising where a middle leader and their team might exert their efforts.

CONCLUDING COMMENT

Leading from the middle is complex and demanding. It can be difficult to gain clarity of thought and direction when putting out daily spot fires and tending to the many demands of students, teachers and other leaders. However, a middle leader can claw back some of the control over their time and energy by investing in their strategic thinking and planning. This chapter has provided middle leaders with ideas and tools that will help in building their strategic leadership capability.

REFERENCES

Australian Institute for Teaching and School Leadership. (2017). *Behaviour Change*. Retrieved from Australian Institute for Teaching and School Leadership. https://www.aitsl.edu.au/lead-develop/develop-yourself-as-a-leader/behaviour-change

Australian Institute for Teaching and School Leadership. (2017, February 8). *Australian professional standard for principals.* https://www.aitsl.edu.au/tools-resources/resource/australian-professional-standard-for-principals

Bendkison, L. (2019). *Leading strategically in educational setting.* The Education Hub. Retrieved January 3, 2023, from https://theeducationhub.org.nz/leading-strategically-in-educational-settings/

Boyle, B., Boyle, T., & Brown, M. (2002). Professional development and management training needs for heads of department in UK secondary schools. *Journal of Educational Administration*, *40*(1), 31–43.

Bryant, D. (2018). Conditions the support middle leaders' work in organisational and system leadership: Hong Kong case studies. *School Leadership and Management*, *39*(5), 415–433.

Carvalho, M., Cabral, I., Verdasca, J., & Alves, J. (2021, October 15). *Strategy and strategic leadership in education: A scoping review.* Frontiers in Education. Retrieved January 3, 2023, from https://www.frontiersin.org/articles/10.3389/feduc.2021.706608/full

Collins. (2022). *Collins English dictionary.* Collins. Retrieved December 31, 2022, from https://www.collinsdictionary.com/dictionary/english/strategic-leadership

Davies, B. J., & Davies, B. (2006). Developing a model for strategic leadership in schools. *Educational Management Administration and Leadership*, *34*(1), 121–139.

Department of Education Queensland School and Region Reviews. (2022). *Strategic leadership for continuous improvement.* Department of Education Queensland.

Grootenboer, P., Edwards-Groves, C., & Ronnerman, K. (2020). *Middle leadership in school: A practical guide for leading learning.* Routledge.

Harvey, J., & Beauchamp, G. (2005). What we're doing, we do musically: Leading and managing music in secondary schools. *Educational Management Administration and Leadership*, *33*(1), 51–67.

Ministry of Education. (2012). *Leading from the middle: Educational leadership for middle and senior leaders.* Ministry of Education.

NSW Department of Education. (2021, November 25). *School excellence in action*. NSW Government – Education. Retrieved December 31, 2022, from https://education.nsw.gov.au/teaching-and-learning/school-excellence-and-accountability/school-excellence-in-action/school-improvement-and-excellence

Robbins, A. (2021). *Middle leadership mastery: A tool kit for subject and pastoral leaders*. Crown House Publishing Limited.

9

MIDDLE LEADERS AS INNOVATORS IN CURRICULUM IMPROVEMENT

Wendy McKay[a] and Donna Pendergast[b]

[a]Department of Education Queensland, Queensland Hospital Education Programs, South Brisbane, QLD, Australia
[b]Griffith University, Nathan, QLD, Australia

ABSTRACT

This chapter is written from the perspective of an experienced middle leader reflecting on what would have been a powerful approach to solving curriculum challenges at the launch of their middle leadership journey. The approach is learning and leading through collaborative inquiry; a process that provides the pathway and direction for a curriculum middle leader (CML) to engage in inquiry to solve a challenge of practice. A CML invests a great deal of time and effort in unpacking and understanding the 'why' of a curriculum challenge. This is achieved through unpacking and understanding the 'how' which led to the challenge, and thus, strong strategic skills are required. Additionally, effective CMLs do not undertake this work in isolation, rather, they build and facilitate a professional learning community (PLC) (Stoll et al., 2006) of curriculum enthusiasts to undertake this journey with them, which requires substantial relational trust.

Keywords: Inquiry cycle; curriculum leadership; relational trust; measures of impact; school improvement; professional learning community

GUIDING QUESTIONS

The following are questions that you should ask yourself before you commence reading this chapter. The questions ask you to consider what you already know and feel about the topic.

1. How do you leverage curriculum problems of practice to spark professional curiosity and drive meaningful professional learning?
2. What experience have you had with using an inquiry approach to leading change? What steps did you take in this cycle?

SETTING THE SCENE

This chapter will demonstrate how a cycle of inquiry can be employed to resolve curriculum challenges at educational sites. At each phase of inquiry, the steps, strategies, and resources used to plan, implement, and review improvement initiatives will be shared and explained. This chapter can be used by curriculum middle leaders (CMLs) as a process for solving challenges of practice, as a framework for building the capability of self or other CMLs, or both. Of critical importance is the message that leading curriculum improvement cannot be undertaken by a CML alone. It takes a professional learning community (PLC) with strong relational trust and effective strategic skills to scan and assess, prioritise, develop and plan, act, and review an improvement initiative to successfully resolve a challenge of practice. This chapter will predominantly focus on the strategies and ideas that proven effective to CML:

- establishing relational trust (scan and assess);
- identifying curriculum challenges of practice (scan and assess);

- strategically prioritising the most significant challenge of practice (prioritise);
- developing an improvement initiative action plan (develop and plan);
- planning to measure impact (develop and plan); and
- measuring impact of implemented improvement initiative (review).

As you read this chapter, you will note that the terms challenge of practice, curriculum challenge, and problem of practice are used interchangeably. They all refer to the curriculum problem that is the focus of the CML's improvement actions.

COLLABORATIVE INQUIRY

Collaborative inquiry is a way for groups of educators to learn from and with each other to improve teacher practice and enhance student learning outcomes (Department of Education (DoE), 2020). In this chapter, the focus remains on curriculum; however, the adapted inquiry cycle process adopted here can be used to successfully scan and assess, prioritise, plan, implement, and review any school-related challenge of practice, see Fig. 9.1.

The collaborative inquiry process begins with the Scan and Assess phase where relevant information about the factors impacting on student outcomes, which, in turn, supports a shared vision on what matters most, are obtained. After scanning the local context widely and analysing data to identify challenges of practice, the Prioritise phase provides the opportunity to narrow the improvement focus. In the next phase, Develop and Plan, the PLC facilitated by the CML collaboratively design an action plan that is guided by the identified challenge of practice and needs of the students and local context. During the Act phase, the team supports one another to implement the plans they have developed. The final phase, Review, involves reflecting on the work the PLC has implemented to understand and evaluate its impact.

Note: The Act phase is not discussed in this chapter.

Fig. 9.1. An Inquiry Cycle.

Source: Adapted from the Queensland Department of Education (DoE, 2020) collaborative inquiry model.

APPLYING AN INQUIRY CYCLE TO RESOLVE A CURRICULUM CHALLENGE

Phase 1: Scan and Assess

a) Establishing a PLC

Building relational trust is critical to success when leading curriculum improvement (Stoll et al., 2006). In this chapter, relational trust can be understood as harmonious respect individual PLC members show each other, as well as a collective understanding about the group's responsibilities and expectations (Cranston, 2011).

Curriculum middle leaders (CMLs) often work and walk alongside executive leaders, other middle leaders, and teachers who are, at times, at their most vulnerable. Perhaps their school has received feedback recommending improvement in one or more aspects of curriculum delivery; their annual report has testified that stakeholders are unhappy with the school's approach to teaching and learning; student achievement data have continued to seesaw across semesters within each school year; or standardised test results have plateaued or declined over time. Often, this news is a catalyst for change, and as such, a PLC of identified curriculum enthusiasts across the school is required to work together through a cycle of inquiry.

Every member of the PLC has a story worth sharing about the school's curriculum journey to date, and every member of the PLC deserves their story to be heard. In building a strong team relationship, the CML listens to learn using effective questioning techniques. Drawing out stories via open and closed curriculum-related questions helps to define issues as the PLC members see them. The use of verbal ('yes', 'I understand', etc.) and non-verbal encouragers (nodding, smiling, etc.) as well as paraphrases (retelling part of the journey in your own words) provides additional clarity and an opportunity for the CML to verify whether they have heard and understood correctly.

The CML will look for occasions to provide warm feedback through highlighting the positives in the school's improvement journey thus far. This type of feedback emphasises the specific areas in which the current curriculum is strong and requires the least amount of trust and, as such, should always be present. The sentence starters below can be an effective way to provide this type of feedback:

1. Attention to detail is evident in the following areas ...
2. It was clear that you worked hard on ...
3. It was interesting when you ...

The CML will also provide cool feedback when analysing the school's curriculum journey or probing for more information. This type of feedback uses critical distance, which means taking a closer look to analyse, probe, and discern. Trust between the CML and PLC members is essential when providing cool feedback. The sentence starters below are to be used gently to delve deeper:

1. I wonder if this fits that ...
2. Have you thought about ...
3. It was unclear to me when you ...

Reflective Question 1

Consider the key ingredients in developing trusting relationships with those for whom you are responsible for building capability. What was the situation? How did you do this? What outcomes did you achieve?

b) Determining a Challenge of Practice

Once a CML has established relation trust with PLC members, the next step is to determine which data will be collected and analysed to ascertain the curriculum challenges. Schools typically have multiple quantitative and qualitative data sets with which to draw from. The CML and PLC cannot possibly know the most significant data sets until all have been reviewed. Data Collection and Analysis Matrix (see Table 9.1) is a very useful tool to carry out this process. It enables the PLC to collect and analyse the following:

- *Student academic data*: Student achievement such as A–E grades, standardised testing results, and/or other whole-school internal assessments.
- *Instructional data*: The curriculum (pedagogical approach), the learning (pedagogical practices), and the learner (teaching and learning strategies).
- *Contextual data*: Knowledge of student backgrounds.
- *Demographic data*: Perceptions about school strengths and challenges (areas of improvement).

Practical Example: Sunny Ridge State School (A Made-up School)

The CML and PLC members at Sunny Ridge State School have identified that A–E English results continue to seesaw across semesters, with higher levels of A and B achievement being awarded in Semester 2.

Over the past two years, multiple improvement initiatives have been introduced to address this challenge of practice. These have included building deeper teacher knowledge and understanding of the curriculum through three levels of planning (whole-school, year level, and unit planning), monthly curriculum conversations with teachers, case management meetings with the CML, and Deputy Principal to build teacher's pedagogical practice, individual mentoring for early career teachers, and instructional coaching across year levels.

Using the Data Collection and Analysis Matrix, the CML, and PLC members have identified a significant challenge of practice: *teachers are still not confident in awarding higher levels of achievement across Semester 1.*

Table 9.1. Data Collection and Analysis Matrix.

Achievement Data	Instructional Data	Contextual Data	Perceptual Data
What do we know about student achievement?	What instructional approaches are being used in classrooms?	Who are our students?	What do stakeholders/ community members perceive to be the strengths and needs in our school?
What do we know about student progress?	What evidence of learning do we capture?	What demographic/ social, etc., data do we capture?	
What dialogic processes do we have in place to understand student achievement and progress?		How does our knowledge and understanding of our students and their needs influence curriculum and pedagogical decisions?	

Source: Authors' own creation.

In the next section, *Prioritising a Challenge of Practice*, the CML and PLC at Sunny Ridge State School will use a fishbone analysis to determine the causes, blockers, and barriers to unpack why teachers are still not confident in awarding higher levels of achievement across Semester 1.

Reflective Question 2

Identify a challenge of practice in your school setting that has persisted regardless of the initiatives implemented to address it. Use the Data Collection and Analysis Matrix to develop an understanding of the challenge of practice from the four data perspectives.

Phase 2: Prioritise a Challenge of Practice

When the Data Collection and Analysis Matrix is used as a tool to identify a challenge of practice, the CML and PLC will unearth concerns, issues, behaviours, or questions that have previously remained unknown. Getting to the core of a challenge of practice is critical to addressing it. Here, a CML can use fishbone analysis (Satya Wacana Christian University, 2016) with the PLC to unpack contributing factors related to an identified challenge.

A fishbone analysis is a graphic tool for analysing cause and effect (Satya Wacana Christian University, 2016). The fishbone's form is like a fish, which has a head (as an effect) and a body in the form of bones (causes of problem or challenge). In Table 9.2, the bones represent the causes, blockers, and barriers that, if resolved, would result in elimination, or substantial reduction, of an identified problem or challenge (Preuss, 2003). This identified problem or challenge becomes the key priority for improvement.

There are five steps of fishbone analysis:

1. Generate a challenge of practice statement.
2. Brainstorm causes, blockers, and barriers.
3. Share and categorise brainstorm.

Table 9.2. Fishbone Analysis.

Step 2. Causes	Step 3. Blockers	Step 4. Barriers	Step 1. Challenge of practice
What might be contributing to the challenge of practice? Why has it happened?	What might stand in the way of improving the challenge of practice? That is, time, space, etc.	What might oppose a solution resolving the challenge of practice? That is, attitude/ behaviour, etc.	Step 5. Categorise causes, blockers, and challenges
Step 2. Causes As above	Step 3. Blockers As above	Step 4. Barriers As above	Step 6. Prioritised challenge of practice goal

Source: Authors' own creation.

4. Reflect and post.
5. Prioritise the challenge of practice.

A fishbone analysis is best undertaken in a space that has a large whiteboard and seating that encourages collaboration. Post-it notes and writing materials are also required. To employ the fishbone analysis tool, a CML and PLC can follow the actions described below.

Step 1: Generate the challenge of practice statement

1. Reflecting on the Data Collection and Analysis Matrix, individually write a broad statement about a challenge of practice. Write clearly on a post-it note.
2. As a group, share all broad statements.
3. As a group, discuss and reach consensus on one statement, that is, 'Teachers are not confident in awarding higher levels of achievement across semester 1 compared to semester 2'.
4. This statement becomes the head of the fish on the template.

Step 2: Brainstorm possible causes

1. As a group, brainstorm potential causes that might contribute to the identified challenge of practice. Write each possible cause on a different post-it note.
2. Place post-it notes in fish on the 'Causes' section.

Step 3: Brainstorm possible blockers

1. As a group, brainstorm potential blockers that might stand in the way of improving the challenge of practice. Write each possible blocker on a different post-it note.
2. Place post-it notes in fish on the 'Blockers' section.

Step 4: Brainstorm possible barriers

1. As a group, brainstorm potential barriers in implementing an improvement initiative. Write each possible challenge on a different post-it note.

2. Place post-it notes in fish on the 'Barriers' section.

Step 5: Share and categorise
As a group:

1. Categorise the causes into related collections and remove unrelated causes.
2. Categorise the blockers into related collections and remove unrelated blockers.
3. Categorise the barriers into related collections and remove unrelated barriers.
4. Reflect on related collections of causes, blockers, and barriers, and on three post-it notes, collaboratively write one statement for each of category encompassing keywords, ideas, themes, concepts, etc.
5. Place the three post-it notes around the head of the fish (fourth column).

Step 6: Reflect and post

1. As group, rewrite the initial identified challenge of practice on a post-it note, that is, Sunny Ridge State School might define their initial curriculum challenge as:

   Teachers are not confident in awarding higher levels of achievement across semester 1 compared to semester 2.

2. On the same post-it note, record the causes, blockers, and barriers identified in Step 5 around the head of the fish using 'because' statements, that is, Sunny Ridge State School might write:

   Teachers are not confident in awarding higher levels of achievement across semester 1 compared to semester 2 because they lack deep knowledge and understanding of achievement standards, because they haven't been provided professional learning opportunities to engage in this work, and because the Head of Curriculum is the gatekeeper of all things curriculum at our school.

Oftentimes, the 'because' statements will be written negatively as that is how they have been recorded in the previous steps. However, once consensus is reached on the challenge of practice as well as the identified causes, blockers, and barriers, it is critical to rewrite the entire statement as a goal using positive language. For example, Sunny Ridge State School could rewrite their challenge as a positive action:

> *To ensure consistency of A-E academic achievement across the school year, we will increase teachers' knowledge and understanding of achievement standards through twice termly moderation opportunities led by a curriculum PLC made up of the CML, Head of Curriculum, and curriculum enthusiasts.*

Step 7: Moving forward to solve the prioritised challenge of practice

The prioritised challenge of practice goal and the steps to reach consensus are shared with the whole school.

Prioritising a challenge of practice is the second step in collaborative inquiry. Several fishbone analyses may be required to fully understand and identify the right challenge of practice, which, if addressed, would have a significant impact on teacher practice and student learning outcomes.

However, a word of advice, 'If everything is a priority, then nothing is!' To move onto the next phase of inquiry, it is crucial that the prioritised challenge of practice is sharp and narrow enough to successfully allow for the development and planning of an improvement initiative.

Reflective Question 3

Review your identified challenge of practice from the previous section. With a colleague, identify one possible cause, blocker, and barrier underpinning the challenge of practice and then collaboratively create a priority goal and action plan.

Phase 3: Develop and Plan

Planning for the successful implementation of an improvement initiative requires a tool to strategically organise and record the steps, responsible officers, required structures or supports, timelines, and necessary resources of an action plan. As a CML, Cole's Professional Funnel for Learning Transference (2012) has proven time and again the foundational framework for developing a well-thought-out action plan because it addresses each of the six phases in the learning transference journey:

- Introduce a highly effective new practice.
- Investigate and receive training in the new practice.
- Trial the new practice in the classroom.
- Reflect and receive feedback to improve practice mastery.
- Add practice to repertoire.
- Help others to adopt the practice.

The learning phases above can be documented in an action planning template. Such an action planning template has been successfully employed by CMLs on varied improvement initiatives. The action plan template should be fore fronted by the prioritised challenge of practice goal. The challenge provides the throughline for proceeding columns in the action plan: related steps, responsible officers, structures or supports, timelines, and resources required to see an improvement initiative through to fruition.

Planning to Measure Impact

At every stage of action planning, it is crucial that the CML and PLC plan for anticipated impact on improved teacher practice and student learning outcomes.

Peter Drucker is famously quoted as saying, 'What gets measured gets improved' (Graves, 2022). This is especially true in schools where multiple improvement initiatives are transpiring at the same time. Additionally, the relationship between professional learning and improvements in teacher practice and student learning outcomes is complicated and includes too many interceding variables to permit simple causal inferences (Guskey, 2002). As such, it is crucial that the PLC prepares for measuring impact at the Develop and Plan phase of an inquiry.

To evaluate the effectiveness of an improvement initiative, evidence should include a balance of qualitative and quantitative measures and should be collected and analysed before (Scan and Assess phase), during (short-term outcomes), and after (overall impact) an improvement initiative has been implemented (Guskey, 2002).

Quantitative methods use numbers for interpreting data and could include:

- Achievement data such as summative assessment data, NAPLAN data (the National Assessment Program – Literacy and Numeracy is an annual assessment for Australian students in Years 3, 5, 7, and 9), diagnostic data, and moderation results.
- Demographic data such as annual school reports.
- Time-series designs such as levels of implementation guides and AITSL Behaviour Change Model (AITSL, 2017).
- Affective outcomes (attitudes and beliefs).
- Psychomotor outcomes (skills and behaviours).
- Aggregate proportion of students receiving A–C grades.

Data for qualitative analysis generally result from the 'coal face' and often include interviews, observations, and documents. Qualitative data collection methods could include:

- Opinion/satisfaction surveys.
- Structured interviews.
- Minutes, conversations, and transcripts from PLCs.
- Teacher reflective journals/notes.

Reflective Question 4

With the same colleague, identify a few qualitative and quantitative measures and collection methods that could be used to monitor and measure the impact of your intervention.

The PLC collects and analyses short-term outcomes at every step of the improvement initiative to monitor progress. The type and length of initiative will determine the kinds of qualitative and quantitative measures required, which often occurs through trial and error. Importantly, knowing what will be monitored supports decision-making around planned activities throughout the act phase (DoE, 2020). As such, it is critical that the PLC commits to regular, timetabled meetings across the initiative to review short-term outcomes and data collection measures and adjust as necessary. Overall, the impact is evaluated at the conclusion of improvement initiative and allows for comparison of baseline and end-point data, which will be discussed further in the following Review phase section.

Phase 5: Review

The Review phase is the final stage of inquiry. While the CML and PLC will monitor progress across the implementation of an improvement initiative, this final phase is more formalised with the group seeking to understand and evaluate overall impact. Here, the CML and PLC aim to identify and understand improvement in teacher practice and student learning outcomes using measures identified in the Develop and Plan phase and then reflect on individual, group, and whole-school learnings to inform future planning (DoE, 2020).

Measures should align directly to anticipated impacts of an improvement initiative and, as stated previously, will include qualitative and quantitative baseline and end-point measures for data comparison. Data comparison is crucial to fortifying the claim that improved outcomes can be attributed to the initiative. There are several methods for comparison-based data, but the simplest method, and one recommended for CMLs building the capability of others, is time-based comparison. Time-based comparison measures improvement, performance, or progress from the beginning (Time A) to the end (Time B) of an improvement initiative.

Let's return to Sunny Ridge State School and consider how time-based comparison could be used to measure the impact of an improvement initiative:

> Improvement Goal: *To ensure consistency of A-E academic achievement across the school year, we will increase teachers' knowledge and understanding of achievement standards through twice termly moderation opportunities led by a curriculum PLC made up of the CML, Head of Curriculum, and curriculum enthusiasts.*

There are four distinct opportunities to measure the impact of an improvement initiative using time-based comparisons at Sunny Ridge State School. The four opportunities measure change in outcomes, progress, processes, and behaviour.

1. Consistency of student achievement data across the school year (outcome):
   Possible measure: Comparison of student achievement data from Semester 1 to Semester 2, across a school year or number of school years.
   Possible measure: Aggregate proportion of students receiving A–C grades from Semester 1 to Semester 2, across a school year or number of school years.

2. Increased teacher knowledge and understanding of achievement standards (progress):
   Possible measure: Pre- and post-testing of teacher knowledge and understanding of achievement standards.
   Possible measure: Structured interviews with teachers.

3. Effectiveness of moderation opportunities twice per term (process):
   Possible measure: Consistency of grading across student work samples.
   Possible measure: Student portfolios of work.

4. Relational trust within PLC (behaviour):
   Possible measure: Plotting behaviour change at the onset, during, and conclusion of an improvement initiative.

Once time-based comparisons have been analysed, the CML and PLC interrogate the degree to which improvements have been made in teacher practice and student learning outcomes to make determinations about whether the improvement initiative has made enough of an impact. If the consensus is such that the improvement initiative has had significant impact on improved outcomes, the team can focus on embedding and sustaining this improvement. However, if the team agrees that improvement does not meet anticipated impact, they may opt to re-enter the Scan and Assess phase using this new data set as the baseline for a subsequent cycle of inquiry.

Reflective Question 5

Consider what types of time-comparison measures you could use to determine the impact of your priority goal and action plan outlined in your Reflective Question 3. Consider both qualitative and quantitative measures to ensure you have a good balance to strengthen the claim that improved outcomes can be attributed to your improvement initiative.

CONCLUSION

Collaborative inquiry provides the pathway and direction for a CML to engage in inquiry to solve a challenge of practice. It can also be used as a framework to build the capability of other middle leaders. Strong relational trust and effective strategic skills are required by the CML to scan and assess, prioritise, develop and plan, act, and review an improvement initiative to successfully resolve an identified challenge of practice. The steps, strategies, and resources presented in this chapter to implement an improvement initiative can be adopted and adapted to suit the local context of the reader's educational setting.

REFERENCES

AITSL (2017). Behaviour Change. Retrieved January 12, 2018, from https://www.aitsl.edu.au/lead-develop/develop-yourself-as-a-leader/behaviour-change

AITSL (2021). Middle Leadership in Australian Schools. Retrieved November 11, 2022, from https://www.aitsl.edu.au/research/spotlights/middle-leadershipin-australian-schools

Cole, P. (2012). *Linking effective professional learning with effective teaching practice*. AITSL.

Cranston, J. (2011). Relational trust: the glue that binds a professional learning community. *Alberta Journal of Educational Research*, *57*(1), 59–72.

Department of Education. (2020). *Collaborative inquiry*. Queensland Government. Retrieved September 24, 2022, from https://learningplace.eq.edu.au/cx/resources/file/2c485fce-bcd3-4252-a246-0f1d2f0aa429/1/resources/inquiry.html

Graves, A. (2022). *What gets managed gets improved*. Silicon Reef. Retrieved Aprile 12, 2023, from https://www.thehrdirector.com/features/big-data/what-gets-measured-gets-improved/#:~:text=This%20was%20recognised%20by%20the,it%20all%20to%20inform%20decisions

Guskey, T. R. (2002). *Does it make a deference? Evaluating professional learning*. Retrieved March 3, 2016, from http://www.ascd.org/publications/educational-leadership/mar02/vol59/num06/Does-It-Make-a-Difference%C2%A2-Evaluating-Professional-Development.aspx

Preuss, P. G. (2003). *School leader's guide to root cause analysis: using data to dissolve problems*. Eye on Education.

Satya Wacana Christian University. (2016). The application of fishbone diagram analysis to improve school quality. *Dinamika Ilmu*, *16*(1), 1–16. P-ISSN: 1411-3031; E-ISSN: 2442-9651.

Stoll, L., Bolam, R., McMahon, A., Wallace, M., & Thomas, S. (2006). Professional learning communities. A review of the literature. *Journal of Educational Change*, 7, 221–258.

10

MIDDLE LEADERS, PROFESSIONAL STANDARDS AND LEADERSHIP GROWTH

Elizabeth Benson[a], Jenny Lewis[b] and Danny Pinchas[c]

[a] *Pivotal Leadership, Gold Coast, QLD, Australia*
[b] *Jenny Lewis and Associates, Springwood, NSW, Australia*
[c] *Australian Institute for Teaching and School Leadership, VIC, Australia*

ABSTRACT

This chapter offers Australian and international insights into leadership development and discusses how aspirant and current middle leaders can use leader and teacher professional standards to foster their professional growth. Standards help inform performance and development planning, and shape feedback and provide a framework for professional learning design. This chapter provides an overview of how systems such as New Zealand, Australia, and Scotland, among others, describe leadership in terms of standards. When used alongside an annual performance and development process, middle leaders can tap into the power of standards to continually sharpen their leadership practice and create a thriving career leading from the middle. Practical guidance is provided for middle leaders to engage with national teacher and leadership standards.

Keywords: Leader standards; teacher standards; middle leader development; leadership growth; international leadership development; leadership continuum; performance and development

GUIDING QUESTIONS

The following are questions that you should ask yourself before you commence reading this chapter. The questions ask you to consider what you already know and feel about the topic.

1. Describe the conversations you have with your line manager about your performance and development? What do they look, sound and feel like?
2. How do you engage with the leadership standards or frameworks provided by your education system to guide your leadership development?

Recognising that middle leadership continues to be formalised and supported in some Australia education sectors, this chapter offers international and national insights and discusses how aspirant and current middle leaders can use leader and teacher professional standards to foster their professional growth. The three authors of this chapter bring unique knowledge and perspective. Danny Pinchas shares his in-depth knowledge of Australian national teacher and leader standards. Jenny explores international leader standards and pathways, and Liz provides an example of how middle leaders can use professional standards to lead their own professional growth.

QUALITY MIDDLE LEADERSHIP MATTERS

Once students enter the school gates, the quality of school leadership is second only to teaching quality in impacting their learning outcomes (Hattie, 2003; Leithwood et al., 2004). School leaders can and should have a big impact on teaching (Robinson et al., 2008). There is an obvious need to ensure all students have quality school leadership around them. For many years, when we thought of school leaders, we thought of principals and deputy principals. Now we recognise the important leadership role of middle leaders and recognise the increasing range of different roles middle leaders have that help improve the learning experience and life outcomes of Australian students.

High-quality school leadership doesn't just happen. Leaders need specific knowledge, skills, and key personal qualities in order to succeed in their leadership actions. Leaders require goals to be set, authentic leadership experiences to occur, targeted and useful feedback and ongoing development opportunities. If we want to identify and develop high-quality school leadership across schools, we need to know precisely what it looks like.

In Australia, we have the benefit of nationally agreed standards for both teachers and principals. The higher career stages (Highly Accomplished and Lead) in the Australian Professional Standards for Teachers (Australian Institute for Teaching and School Leadership (AITSL), 2011) provide the platform for expert teachers and aspirational school leaders to improve the teaching practice of other teachers and embark on a leadership journey. The Australian Professional Standard for Principals (AITSL, 2014) describes the knowledge and skills required for successful leadership of a school. Many middle leaders currently use both sets of standards (often with frustration) to reflect on their leadership practice and plan their next steps in development. Effectively, they are creating their own ad-hoc development framework that is disjointed and disconnected from the other tens of thousands middle leaders. Table 10.1 provides an overview of the national standards for teachers and principals.

Professional standards for middle leaders will help the education sector in several ways. Standards would articulate a shared understanding of what leaders should know and do at key junctures in their career and across various contexts. They would help raise the status of leadership in schools and therefore the wider profession, a focus of the National Teacher Workforce Action Plan (Department for Education (DfE), 2022c).

Table 10.1. An Overview of the National Standards for Teachers and Principals.

Australian Professional Standards for Teachers				**The Australian Professional Standard for Principals**
Graduate	Proficient →	High Accomplished →	Lead →	Principal
		Formal recognition achieved through an application and evidence of practice		
• Professional knowledge				• Leadership requirements
• Professional practice				• Professional practices
• Professional engagement				

Source: Authors' own creation.

Standards outline a common set of expectations and provide a common language with which to describe them. While they are used to evaluate performance, they have most transformational power (AITSL, 2016) when used formatively and owned by the profession. Standards help inform career development, performance and development planning, shape feedback so it is targeted and provide a framework for professional learning design and collaboration to improve practice. Middle leaders standards would also underpin tools and resource development, helping middle leaders navigate the multitude of development opportunities and select the most appropriate for their needs, based on a validated body of evidence.

Whether a middle leader has a role that is primarily pedagogical, student-based or in program leadership (AITSL, 2022), standards can help by taking out the mystery of the leadership skills and knowledge they apply. Standards for middle leaders would provide a framework for career progression into senior leadership, as well as support ongoing development for career middle leaders with no aspirations for principalship. They will help validate and showcase the significant impact middle leaders have on their colleagues and students, both within the profession and over time to the broader community.

Middle leaders can use standards to shape their leadership and their leadership career. Standards make explicit the connections and next steps between teaching, school leadership and even into system leadership. They can help middle leaders create portfolios of evidence to understand and communicate their impact, for both internal (e.g. performance and development planning) and for external (e.g. job applications and accreditation) purposes.

WHAT IS HAPPENING INTERNATIONALLY FOR MIDDLE LEADER GROWTH AND DEVELOPMENT? FINDING IDEAS AND RESOURCES FOR YOUR DEVELOPMENT PLANS

International research has recognised the pivotal role that middle leaders play in school improvement, professional learning, curriculum development, leadership development, and promoting change to improve student outcomes in schools (Bryant & Walker, 2022; Fleming, 2014; Harris & Jones, 2017; Highfield & Robertson, 2016).

While the term 'middle leader' and associated research is limited to a few education jurisdictions including England, Israel, New Zealand, Scotland, Sweden, and Norway, it is recognised that many education jurisdictions commit to increasing leadership density across the school and the growth and development of those seeking a career pathway to senior leadership. Several education jurisdictions including Canadian provinces, for example, Alberta and Ontario, Hong Kong, Singapore, the United States, and Wales have focused on supporting those aspiring to assistant principal and equivalent roles and have invested in the provision of formal preparation programs and credentials.

Like Australia, several education jurisdictions have introduced a leadership continuum that generally provides a career pathway from teacher leadership to middle leadership to senior leadership.

For the aspiring or middle leader, it is useful to compare how other education systems view the development of leading capability over a career. In this next section, a brief overview is provided of the pathways and standards in Scotland, England, and New Zealand. While you are reading these brief descriptions, you may wish to reflect on how the path to (and possibly through) middle leadership is viewed by other education systems.

Scotland

In 2021, the General Teaching Council for Scotland, in collaboration with the ministry and profession, designed and implemented a professional standards architecture that promotes teacher professionalism in Scotland as a 'way of being' (General Teaching Council for Scotland, 2023a). Along with professional standards for teachers, there are professional standards headteachers and Scotland college lecturers (General Teaching Council for Scotland, 2021) (see Table 10.2).

The suite of school-based professional standards is underpinned by the interdependent themes of professional values and professional commitment, learning for sustainability, and leadership, similar to the Australian Professional Standards for Teachers Domains of Professional Knowledge, Practice and Engagement. This suite provides a shared language and curriculum for professional growth, a benchmark for professional competency, career pathways and a process for recruitment, and selection.

Table 10.2. General Teaching Council for Scotland Professional Standards Architecture.

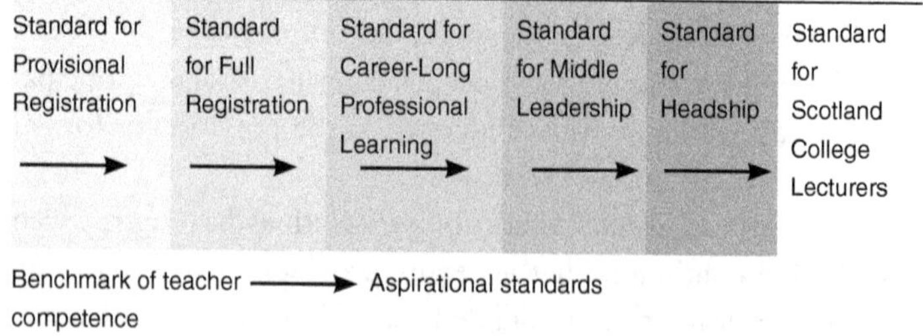

Standard for Provisional Registration →	Standard for Full Registration →	Standard for Career-Long Professional Learning →	Standard for Middle Leadership →	Standard for Headship →	Standard for Scotland College Lecturers

Benchmark of teacher competence → Aspirational standards

Source: Authors' own creation.

The Standard for Middle Leadership focuses on leadership of, and for learning, teacher leadership, and working collegially to build leadership capacity in others (General Teaching Council for Scotland, 2023b). Interestingly, in Scotland, the middle leader standards are underpinned by a set of professional values: social justice, trust and respect and integrity. It is these values that encourage a middle leader to reflect and make connections between values and actions (or leading practices) and commit to professional learning over their whole career.

Education Scotland provides a suite of professional development programs explicitly mapped to and aligned with the Professional Standards, including the Aspiring to Middle Leadership Program to develop understanding of the roles and skills required in a middle leadership position. Education Scotland also provides the Middle Leaders Leading Change program which is designed to develop skills, knowledge and confidence in the use of coaching and reflection and the use of an enquiring stance when planning and leading change and addressing anti-racism in the workplace and community.

New Zealand

The formal role of middle leader has been a focus of New Zealand research, policy and practice since 2012. In 2018, the Education Council of Aotearoa authorised the development of the Educational Leadership Capability Framework which provides a leadership continuum and career pathway from expert teachers to leading

Table 10.3. Education Council Education Leadership Capabilities Architecture: New Zealand.

	2018 Educational Leadership Capability Framework		
Standards for the Teaching Profession	Expert teacher, leadership of curriculum or initiative	Leading teams →	Leading organisations →

Source: Authors' own creation.

teams (middle leadership) to organisational leadership for school and system leaders (see Table 10.3) (Education Council, 2018; Ministry of Education, 2023).

For middle leaders, the Educational Leadership Capability Framework provides a high-level description of nine educational leadership capabilities, what these capabilities look like at each career level in practice and illustrations of what these practices look like in different contexts.

Many of the themes discussed by middle leaders in this book reflect the New Zealand Education Leadership Capabilities:

1. Building and sustaining high trust relationships.
2. Building and sustaining collective leadership and professional community.
3. Strategically thinking and planning.
4. Evaluating practices in relation to outcomes.
5. Adept management of resources to achieve vision and goals.
6. Attending to their own learning as leaders and their own well-being.
7. Embodying the organisation's values and showing moral purpose, optimism, agency, and resilience.
8. Contributing to the development and well-being of education beyond their organisation.

And like the Australian Professional Standards for Teachers, they include a focus on knowledge and understanding of culturally responsive practice.

Interestingly, for middle leader development, the Education Leadership Capabilities Framework provides reflection questions to help the middle leaders guide their development, for example, Why did I find this challenging? Who or what could help me develop my skills/knowledge in this capability (Education Council, 2018)?

England

The England Department of Education (DfE) mandates a national continuum of professional qualifications that support the professional

Table 10.4. DfE National Professional Qualifications (NPQs) Architecture: England.

DfE Teachers' Standards	DfE NPQs				
	Early years leadership	NPQ specialist areas of teaching • Leading teacher development • Leading teaching • Leading behaviour and culture • Leading literacy	School senior leadership →	School headship	School executive leadership →

Source: Authors' own creation.

development of teachers and school and system leaders (see Table 10.4). For educators leading from the middle, the Middle Leader Qualification can guide the development of their expertise in specialist areas of teaching practice. These specialist areas include the following:

1. Leading teacher development.
2. Leading teaching and learning of a subject, year group, or school phase.
3. Leading behaviour and culture in which staff and pupils can thrive.
4. Leading literacy across the whole school, year group, key stage, or phase.

For middle leaders who wish to progress to senior leadership, there are qualifications that can be completed in senior leadership, headship, executive leadership and early years leadership (DfE, 2022a, 2022b).

Be curious and broaden the range of resources you access to develop your leading practices. Choose one or more of the education systems discussed in this chapter and spend time scanning the tools and resources available to you. Once you have read the next section in this chapter, you will be able to incorporate some of the ideas and resources from these websites in your growth and development plan.
England: www.bestpracticenet.co.uk
New Zealand: https://www.educationalleaders.govt.nz/
Scotland: www.gtcs.org.uk
Australia: www.aitsl.edu.au

Fig. 10.1. Finding Interesting Resources for Your Growth and Development.

All four education systems discussed in this chapter provide useful resources for middle leaders to reflect on their leading practices and design a development strategy for themselves. Middle leaders in one jurisdiction are encouraged to look at the resources provided in others to find examples of leading practice across a wide range of common middle leader responsibilities, for example, designing professional learning for teachers, leading with strategic intent, developing a faculty culture or leading with cultural sensitivity. Fig. 10.1 provides links to relevant jurisdiction resources.

USING LEADERSHIP STANDARDS TO FUEL YOUR GROWTH AND DEVELOPMENT: AN EXAMPLE

As noted earlier in this chapter, Australian educators have access to a wide range of national, state and school policies, processes and resources to support them to fuel a meaningful and satisfying leadership career. The affirms that 'working across both the Teacher Standards and Principal Standard is important for reflecting on improving leadership practice' (AITSL, 2017b).

Like many middle leaders, Liz has carved out a lengthy career in school and system middle leadership. In some contexts, Liz was well supported by school leaders and culture that valued annual performance and development processes. In other contexts, Liz's professional development was left to her to drive. What Liz has learnt is that in no matter what context, the teacher standards and leader standards are an excellent support for her to take ownership and responsibility for her growth.

HOW CAN A MIDDLE LEADER USE TEACHER AND LEADERSHIP STANDARDS TO SHAPE THEIR LEADERSHIP DEVELOPMENT?

Using an appreciative inquiry frame (Moore, 2019) as the foundation for her own development has meant that Liz can use the resources and tools available in each educational context to drive her leadership career forward. By starting with reflection (Discover) to gain insight into her leading and teaching strengths as well as her dreams for both, Liz can position (Design) her performance and development plan to meet her development needs as well as the performance demands of the school (Destiny).

Reflecting on her approach, Liz has generated a bank of appreciative inquiry questions a middle leader can use to take ownership and responsibility for their own development. Table 10.5 sets out these questions using a generic performance and development process.

Many systems provide tools to encourage the middle leader to reflect on their teaching and leading and to identify development goals and actions. For example, Liz has used the AITSL Principal Standard Reflection Tool (AITSL, 2017b) and the Teacher Self-Assessment Tool (AITSL, 2017a) for many years, in different roles and contexts. Liz ensures that she uses both to capture her current leadership (Discover) and teaching strengths and identify goals (Dream) for her development in both areas. Liz always starts by completing the self-reflection tools before engaging in any conversation about development goals, so the process is informed by evidence. Liz captures her growth (Destiny) over time by saving the visual representation produced at the end of each reflection survey. When viewed chronologically, Liz can see her growth as a leader and teacher, as well as how the changing leadership capabilities needed for success in various leadership roles, for example, leading a faculty or a whole school program.

Table 10.5. An Appreciative Inquiry Approach to Middle Leader Performance and Development Created by Liz Benson.

Appreciative Inquiry Phase	Generic Education Performance and Development Process	Appreciative Inquiry Questions for a Middle Leader
Discovery 'Appreciating the best of'	• Use of system tools to self-reflect against leading and teaching standards • Feedback from line manager, colleagues, and students • Use of evaluative data to identify performance against school strategic goals • Identifying strengths to shift perceptions of leadership from deficit thinking	• What are my strengths as a leader? • What are my strengths as a teacher? • What do my students enjoy about my teaching practice? • What do my colleagues and team appreciate about my leading practice?
Dream 'What might be'	• Conversations with line manager about insights gained from reflection • Line manager uses positive questions to unlock possibilities in development conversations • Reflective alignment of strengths against school strategic goals	• Where (or how) will my leadership strengths most effectively support the achievement of school strategic goals? • What do I want to get better at when I lead? • Where do I want my leadership journey to take me this year, in 5 years, in 10 years?

Design
'What should be'
	• Performance and development conversations to design a way to achieve goals
	• Identification of the next steps in leadership development using standards that describe the growth in leadership practice
	  ○ Using system role descriptions, for example, head of department, to identify what is needed to undertake a middle leadership role
	  ○ SMART goal setting
	  ○ Career goal setting
	• Co-design with line manager an individualised professional development plan to fuel leadership growth
		• What leadership skills and knowledge do I need to lead and teach …
		  ○ for my career goals
		  ○ in my current role
		  ○ to contribute to the achievement of school strategic goals?
		• What pedagogical and curriculum skills and knowledge do I need to lead and teach?
		• What skills and knowledge do I need to achieve my career goals?
		• What skills and knowledge do I need to support the achievement of school strategic goals?

(*Continued*)

Table 10.5. (*Continued*)

Appreciative Inquiry Phase	Generic Education Performance and Development Process	Appreciative Inquiry Questions for a Middle Leader
Destiny 'What will be'	• End of performance and development cycle conversations, where evidence is used to determine goal achievement; and leadership and teaching growth	• What will I look, sound, and feel like when I am leading and teaching at my best? • What professional learning did I engage in and how has it helped me grow as a leader/teacher? • How has my teaching practice evolved this school year? • How has my leadership grown since the start of the school year? • How has my leadership contributed to the achievement of school goals?

Source: Authors' own creation.

While formal reflection tools (such as from AITSL) are useful, unless they have 360-degree feedback capability, they are only providing insights based on self-reflection. It is very useful for a middle leader to also gather feedback that might provide perceptions into their leading and teaching from their colleagues, line manager, team, students, and community. A middle leader can choose to purchase a commercial 360 tool, use the AITSL 360 Reflection Tool or ask their leadership coach to seek 360 feedback from trusted colleagues and students. A quick and simple method Liz has used previously is to ask four questions:

1. What should I start doing?
2. What should I stop doing?
3. What should I continue to do?
4. What are my blind spots that I need to know about to support you?

Liz maps insights gained from these four questions against leadership standards to add depth to discovering and appreciating the best of her leadership. No matter what 360 method is employed, it is important for the middle leader to feedback to the respondents what they learnt about their leadership and what actions they will take for their development.

WHAT PRACTICAL SUPPORT DO LEADERSHIP STANDARDS PROVIDE MIDDLE LEADERS?

The advantages of engaging with system provided professional standards such as the Principal Standard and Teacher Standards include the following:

- they help locate current leadership skills, styles and practices within a leadership model or framework that has been rigorously developed and tested;
- reports that are produced from the associated reflection tools help track development over time. This can also create a sense of momentum in a career that can span many years. This is

very useful for middle leaders whose career spans states and systems;

- reflection tools help to identify leadership and teaching strengths prior to setting a goal for future growth and identifying professional learning needed;
- they provide a common language for discussing development with other leaders within a system/school (including your line manager);
- they help identify what leadership skills, knowledge and practices are needed to prepare for the next phase of leadership. Using the language and evidence from system reflection tools is useful when advocating for desired professional learning; and
- they can provide language and evidence for sharing leadership stories and successes, for example, when mentoring other teachers or advocating for yourself in a job application.

THE CHALLENGE ... OR THE FUTURE ...

Professional standards for leaders are a significant feature of many education systems across the world. Middle leaders can use the standard descriptions and the associated tools and resources to take ownership of their leadership development.

At the time of writing this chapter, AITSL commenced working in partnership with the Queensland Department of Education to develop, validate and trial professional standards for middle leaders. It is hoped that these standards will then be adopted nationally.

To be effective, standards for middle leaders should clearly connect with the teacher and principal standards and articulate increasing levels of proficiency balanced with the need to be useful across contexts. They will need buy-in from middle leaders and other members of the profession, primarily from principals and system/sector leaders. They need to be communicable – easily shared with and understood by teachers. They will need to be used in a range of ways and backed by supporting resources to help bring the words to life. Most importantly, they will need to be owned by middle leaders themselves.

REFERENCES

Australian Institute for Teaching and School Leadership. (2011). *Australian professional standards for teachers*. AITSL.

Australian Institute for Teaching and School Leadership. (2014). *Australian professional standard for principals, and the leadership profiles*. AITSL.

Australian Institute for Teaching and School Leadership. (2016). *Final report – Evaluation of the Australian professional standards for teachers*. AITSL in partnership with The University of Melbourne.

Australian Institute for Teaching and School Leadership. (2017a). *Leading for impact*. Retrieved January 15, 2023, from https://www.aitsl.edu.au/lead-develop/build-leadership-in-Australian-schools/leading-for-impact-online

Australian Institute for Teaching and School Leadership. (2017b). *Reflect on your leadership*. Retrieved January 15, 2023, from https://www.aitsl.edu.au/lead-develop/develop-yourself-as-a-leader/reflect-on-your-leadership

Australian Institute for Teaching and School Leadership. (2022). *Spotlight – Middle leadership in Australian schools*. https://www.aitsl.edu.au/research/spotlights/middle-leadership-in-australian-schools

Bryant, D. A., & Walker, A. (2022). Principal-designed structures that enhance middle leaders' professional learning. *Educational Management Administration & Leadership*, 1–20. https://doi.org/10.1177/17411432221084154

Department for Education. (2022a, December 16). *Guidance national professional qualifications (NPQs)*. https://www.gov.uk/government/publications/national-professional-qualifications-npqs-reforms/national-professional-qualifications-npqs-reforms

Department for Education. (2022b, December 20). *National professional qualifications frameworks: From autumn 2021*. www.gov.uk

Department for Education. (2022c). *The national teacher workforce action plan*. The Australian Government.

Education Council. (2018). *Educational leadership capability framework*. https://teachingcouncil.nz/assets/Files/Leadership-Strategy/Leadership_Capability_Framework.pdf

Fleming, P. (2014). *Successful middle leadership in secondary schools: A practical guide to subject and team effectiveness*. Routledge.

General Teaching Council for Scotland. (2021). *GTC Scotland professional standards 2021: Professional standards side by side comparison*. https://www.gtcs.org.uk/wp-content/uploads/2021/09/professional-standards-side-by-side-comparison.pdf

General Teaching Council for Scotland. (2023a). *Professional Standards*. https://www.gtcs.org.uk/professional-standards/

General Teaching Council for Scotland. (2023b). *Self-evaluation wheel: Standard for middle leadership 2021*. https://www.gtcs.org.uk/wp-content/uploads/2021/09/self-evaluation-wheel-standard-for-middle-leadership.pdf

Harris, A., & Jones, M. (2017). Middle leaders matter: reflections, recognition, and renaissance. *School Leadership & Management*, *37*(3), 213–216.

Hattie, J. (2003). Teachers make a difference: What is the research evidence? Paper presented to Australian Council for Educational Research Annual Conference, October 19–21, Melbourne.

Highfield, C., & Robertson, J. (2016). *Professional learning and development facilitation practices that enhance secondary school middle leader effectiveness*. Australian Association for Research in Education.

Leithwood, K., Louis, K. S., Anderson, S., & Wahlstrom, K. (2004). *How leadership influences student learning*. Center for Applied Research and Educational Improvement, University of Minnesota.

Ministry of Education. (2023). *Educational leadership capability framework*. https://www.educationalleaders.govt.nz/Leadership-development/Professional-information/Leadership-capability-framework

Moore, C. (2019). *What is appreciative inquiry? (Definition, examples & model)* (p. 27). Retrieved January 15, 2023, from https://positivepsychology.com/appreciative-inquiry/#appreciative-inquiry

Robinson, V. M. J., Lloyd, C. A., & Rowe, K. J. (2008). The impact of leadership on student outcomes: An analysis of the differential effects of leadership types. *Educational Administration Quarterly*, *44*(5), 635–674. https://doi.org/10.1177/0013161X08321509

FINAL THOUGHTS: MIDDLE LEADERS DEVELOPING MIDDLE LEADERS – WHERE TO NEXT

We started this book with the premise that middle leadership is a time for developing middle leader identity and ended with a look at how middle leaders can use the professional standards provided by systems for leadership growth and development. In-between middle leaders have shared their strategies and ideas for leading with impact.

We hope that like each middle leader who has contributed to this book, you are empowered to find your voice and share your success and struggles of leading from the middle with your colleagues. As a profession, we are on the path to untangling the complexities of middle leadership, and we believe the chapter authors in this book have provided educators with a little more insight into what middle leaders do and how they do it.

As editors, we discussed the idea of selecting key gems of information from each chapter as advice to middle leaders and other readers. However, we soon realised that these would represent our preferences and not, necessarily, yours as readers. Each chapter includes leadership advice from a selection of world-class middle leaders, leadership researchers, and practitioners. We concluded that this book is a 'goldmine' of wisdom that should be mined by our readers and that it is best if you select what is relevant for you in your educational circumstances. We hope that you will 'dig deep' and that your students benefit from the wisdom you derive from these pages.

We wish you a bright and productive future as an influential educational leader.

Liz, Patrick, and Barbara

INDEX

Printed in the USA
CPSIA information can be obtained
at www.ICGtesting.com
JSHW061357110424
61007JS00013B/173

9 781837 530854

"With its diverse perspectives from across Australia, this book is an invaluable companion for anyone navigating the muddy waters of middle leading. I wish I had this treasure during my own middle leadership journey!"

- Lauren Sayer, Director, The Victorian Curriculum and Assessment Authority

"It will assist you to unravel the challenges of getting the best from your organisation's middle layer."

- Bill Lowe, Responsible for the design and delivery of Education Leadership in the Education, MA at Newman University, Birmingham, UK.

There is a lack of studies and practical resources available for supporting the professional development of middle leaders. Based on research and consultations with influential school middle leaders, *Middle Leadership in Schools* presents ideas and actions designed specifically to stimulate and enhance educators leading from the middle, as a catalyst to enable them to do what they do with greater influence and impact.

Each chapter focuses on a challenge of leading from the middle, drawing from successful practice and case studies whilst providing contemporary research and practical strategies to guide middle leaders to success.

Offering a unique combination of academic rigour and practical advice, *Middle Leadership in Schools* is essential reading for teachers, current and aspiring middle leaders, school leaders, and postgraduate students studying educational leadership.

Elizabeth Benson is an educator, school middle leader and founder of Pivotal Leadership, offering coaching and professional development for middle leaders. In 2018, Liz established the ACELQ Pivotal People Middle Leaders network, facilitating networking and learning opportunities for aspiring and middle leaders.

Patrick Duignan is Emeritus Professor at Australian Catholic University, Australia, life member of the Australian Council for Educational Leaders, and Director of Leading to Inspire.

Barbara Watterston is CEO of the Australian Council for Educational Leaders. She has a long and distinguished career in education and has held several executive leadership positions across Australia within the education and not-for-profit community sectors.

ISBN 978-1-83753-085-4

Cover design:
Mike Hill
Image base:
@xorosho
via Getty Images